THE *Best* OF THE SOUTHWEST

The Canyonlands Travel Guide for a One Week(or Two Week) Trip of a Lifetime

STEVE CARR

Cover Photo is of the Garden of Eden in the Needles Section of Canyonlands National Park by Southwest photographer extraordinaire Dan Norris @ http://www.dannorrisphotography.com/

Maps graciously provided by Dr. John Crossley
@ The American Southwest @ http://www.americansouthwest.net/

Map route created by my personal IT Wizard (and lovely wife) Inna Young.

Cover design by Steve Carr

 ISBN 978-1-54392-894-5 eBook 978-1-54392-895-2

DEDICATION

This book is dedicated to the love of my life, Inna Young, who supported me with this book and assisted me with numerous technical issues that popped up along the way. And to my old friend Jimmy Martin who was my trusty sidekick in August 2017, when we returned to the Southwest to verify the recommendations in this book. And to all my Southwest friends who keep me coming back for more.

Table of Contents

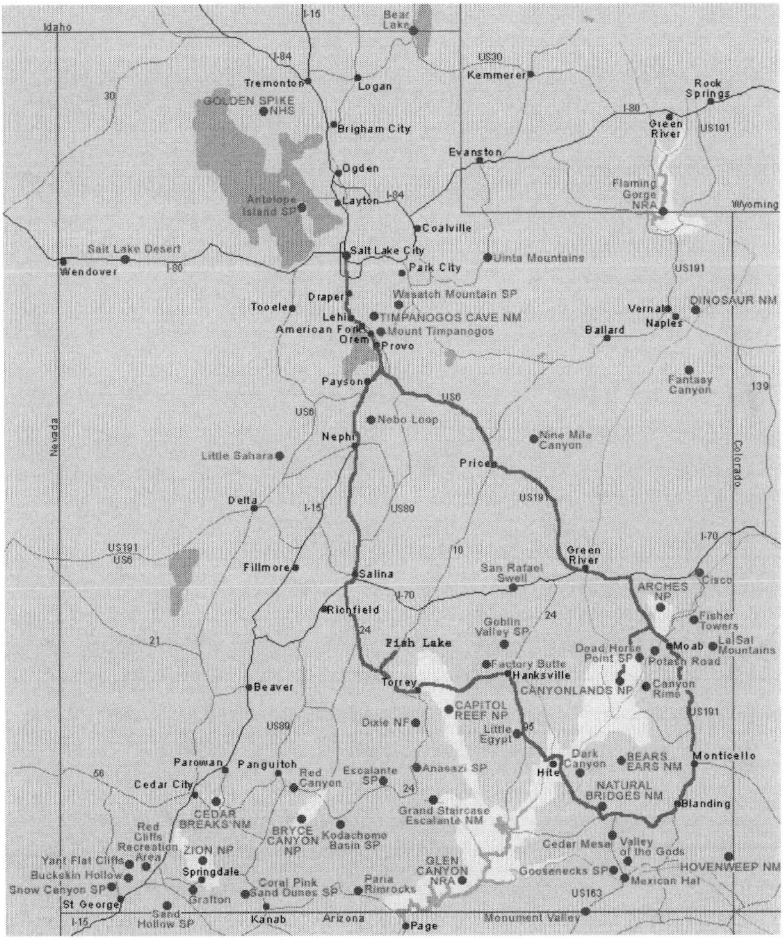

Seven Day Trip - Map

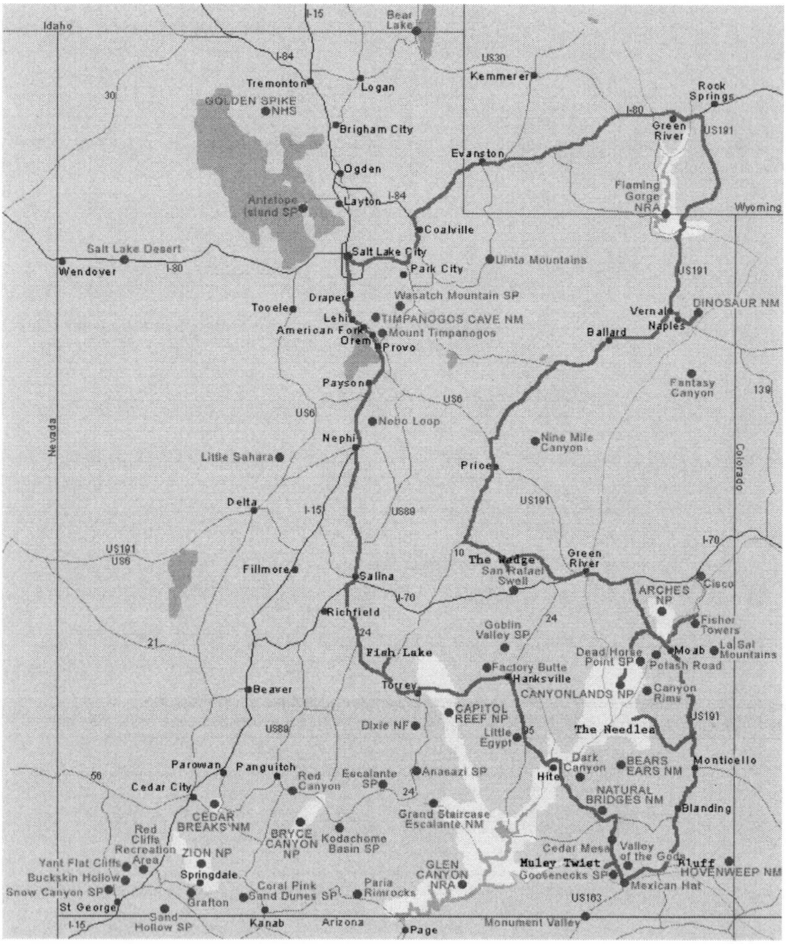

Fourteen Day Trip - Map

ITINERARY - Seven Day

- Day One – Fly to Salt Lake and Drive to Green River, Utah
- Day Two – Arches National Park
- Day Three – Canyonlands National Park - Island in the Sky
- Day Four – Natural Bridges National Monument
- Day Five – Little Wild Horse Slot Canyon and Capitol Reef National Park
- Day 6 – Capitol Reef National Park
- Day Seven – Capitol Reef, Small Mormon Towns, Fish Lake, Salt Lake City & Fly Home

ITINERARY - Fourteen Day

- Day One – Fly to Salt Lake and Drive to Green River, Wyoming
- Day Two – Flaming Gorge
- Day Three – Dinosaur National Monument
- Day Four – The Wedge and San Rafael River
- Day Five – Arches National Park
- Day Six – Colorado River Trip
- Day Seven – Canyonlands National Park - Island in the Sky
- Day Eight – Negro Bill Canyon and Canyonlands - The Needles
- Day Nine – Day Ten – Blanding, Bluff, Mexican Hat, and the San Juan River
- Day Ten – Natural Bridges National Monument
- Day Eleven– Little Wild Horse Slot Canyon and Capitol Reef National Park
- Day Twelve – Capitol Reef National Park
- Day Thirteen – Chimney Rock, Small Mormon Towns, Fish Lake, and the Salt Lake Valley
- Day Fourteen – Temple Square and Fly Home

SEVEN DAYS ON THE ROAD

PLANNING YOUR TRIP

Getting There

I usually fly to Salt Lake City after work on a Friday, so I can save a day of holiday leave and utilize two weekends for the trip. You can book your flight through a website like Kayak to get the best deal, but I always fly **Southwest Airlines**. They are the biggest airline in the Southwest, hence the name. You can expect to pay about $500 per person round-trip (RT) from the east coast. Southwest is the only airline that does not charge for the first checked bag or your carry-on bag.

- Arrive in Salt Lake City by **3PM** because you have a long drive after your flight.

What to Bring

- Clothes for warm and cold weather for hiking, camping & checking out towns
- Wool cap & gloves
- Sweater or fleece top
- Swimsuit
- Towel
- Hiking shoes
- Casual Shoes
- Flip flops or sport sandals
- Rain gear (good poncho)
- Sunscreen (Bullfrog Waterproof)

- Glasses/Contacts/Sunglasses
- Hat & bandana
- Quart water bottles (4)
- Moist towelettes to clean yourself
- Doc Bronner's soap + washcloth + large beach towel
- Day pack or large hip pack
- Telescoping walking stick
- Matches or a lighter
- Resealable plastic baggies
- Smartphone
- Camera
- Tablet/iPad
- Chargers
- Earbuds or headphones
- Plug adaptors
- Small flashlight
- Earplugs
- Small lock and metal cord to secure your luggage in the trunk
- Good book
- Airline reservations
- Driver's License or passport
- Rental car voucher
- Hotel confirmation
- Cash ($20 bills)
- Credit/Debit cards
- Health insurance/medical records
- First-aid kit
- Notepad & Pen

- Tissues
- Travel alarm/watch
- Sewing kit
- Good maps (many can be downloaded off the **Avenza** website an app that provides geopdf's topographic maps that work without an Internet connection and which can be downloaded to an Android or iPhone. ***https://www.topo-gps.com/***

Camping Gear

- Tent (lightweight)
- Inflatable pillow
- Sleeping bag rated for 0 degrees (the temperature rating is usually at least 25 degrees warmer than it really is because they assume you are wearing lots of clothes)
- Garbage bags
- Thick ground pad, preferably a Thermarest air mattress
- A reflective space blanket to use under your tent as a ground pad
- An absorbent camping towel to wipe the dew off your gear in the morning
- Moist towelettes to clean yourself
- Doc Bronner's soap + washcloth + large beach towel
- Toilet Paper
- Water purification tablets
- Small shovel to dig your 7"-deep cat hole for human waste if you are primitive camping
- Several stuff sacks to store gear
- Head lamp
- Spare batteries
- Lawn chair & Cooler (buy @ Walmart)

Another option, is to try the **Lost Campers** company who will rent you a small camper RV (RV rentals usually will run you about $100 a day, not including gas). They have an office in Salt Lake City and might be just the ticket if you would just like to rent a bed on wheels that would allow you to avoid costly hotels or carrying a lot of camping equipment.

If you want to camp and don't want to schlep your heavy camping gear through airports, there is a nationally-renowned rental company in Salt Lake City called **REI** that will rent you a tent, sleeping bag, ground pads and everything you will need to sleep out under the Milky Way.
https://www.rei.com/stores/salt-lake-city.html

When to Go

The best time to visit the Southwest is in the spring or the fall. Summers can be excruciatingly hot, and winters are bitterly cold. Spring temperatures are nice but there are three disadvantages: it can be windy, the night time temperatures are still chilly, and the water in places like Lake Powell or the Green River will still be cold from the spring runoff. **Fall (September - October) is the best time for your visit**. The lakes and rivers are still warm, and the swimming is great. The night time temperatures are delightful. There are no bugs. The weather tends to be nice and dry. And the aspen leaves turn the mountains a bright yellow. So, I would book your trip in September, after the school kids and families have all gone home.

Please keep in mind that regardless of the season, a change in elevation can change the weather dramatically. A good rule of thumb is this: **the higher the elevation, the colder and stormier it can be**. When I was doing the recon for this book in August of 2017, it was 100 degrees down at the lower elevations in places like Arches, but I ran into snow driving over the Manti-La Sal and Uinta mountains.

Rental Cars

- You should rent a **Sport Utility Vehicle**. They are not that much more expensive than a passenger car and they will give you lots of space for coolers, lawn chairs, food, and luggage. And given that you will be going off-road at times, it is always wise to have a vehicle with high clearance. SUV Rental (7 days) - **$500** (does not include gas).
- **Salt Lake City International Airport offers a variety of rental car providers and convenient access to rental car services. Rental car counters are located on the ground floor of the parking garage, directly across from the terminal buildings. For assistance, contact the airport ground transportation desks at (801) 575-2310 or (801) 575-2312.**

Accommodations and Meals

The hotels and restaurants listed in this book are not necessarily the best places to stay or eat. But these are the places where I stop. I chose them because they are clean, conveniently located, and reasonably priced. I assume that the travelers using this book are not looking to spend a lot of money. If you like, you can probably find more lavish accommodations or fancier places to dine. I have tried to strike a **reasonable balance between expensive and cheap**. So, you can find other options on either end of the cost scale. That said, in the smaller and more isolated towns, the choices are limited, and my selections are going to be your best bet. But in places like Moab, you can spend a lot more to eat and stay in luxury. In short, my recommendations are for the **average traveler on a limited budget**, trying to keep their costs down while still enjoying themselves.

How to Use This Book

There are some great Southwest guide books on the market. But they all share one common, and rather annoying, trait: **THEY OFFER TOO MANY CHOICES**. If your guide truly knows the area in question, then why do they fill their books with a lot of superfluous information?

The ***Best of the Southwest*** series gives you **very few choices**. I lived in the Southwest and explored the Canyonlands for fifteen years. I know it like the back of my hand. I know the best places to eat, stay, visit, and hike. And if you were doing the trip with me, we would follow my itinerary to the letter. That's why you paid for the book: to find out the **best** things to do and how to do them in a logical way, given the limited time you will be vacationing.

Rather than give you a list of restaurants in each town organized by cuisine and price, I tell you **where I would eat**. And instead of listing all the hikes in a park organized by their difficulty and length, I steer you to the **best hikes**. **Hotels are always a subjective and budgetary consideration**. I don't spend a lot of time in the hotel. I sleep there and then leave and maybe use the pool. So, I don't need luxury. You might feel different about that, and that's fine.

In the end, this is **your** vacation and you should do whatever you like. If you don't feel like doing a hike or eating where I suggested, that's cool. Your mission is to have **fun**! Don't let the book turn your trip into a job. Take time to relax and enjoy wherever you may be. If you follow the book step-by-step, you will have a great time. But **flexibility** is always the key to enjoyable exploration. And ***exploration is always about the journey, not the destination***.

I have provided handy **URL links** to each attraction listed in this book, so you can find additional information and get the **up-to-date prices** and conditions. But please keep in mind that the **links were created in 2017**. Links die. Businesses close. The Southwest is fluid and always changing. So, before you leave on your trip, you should check the links to make sure they are still valid, and if they aren't, make a note of the new ones.

The seven days and fourteen days trips are **not** identical. In most respects they are quite different. For instance, the first four days of the longer trip cover a vast area that will not be visited by those doing the shorter trip. But some of the days do mirror one another (Arches, Canyonlands - Island in the Sky, Little Wild Horse Slot Canyon, and some of Capitol Reef), so there is some unavoidable repetition.

As an added bonus, I am going to fill in your days with many helpful **Insider Tips** that will give you information about the places you visit that few people know about.

And I will also show you how to **save your hard-earned money!**

So, just load this trusty guide onto your smartphone or iPad, follow my handy dandy directions, and the Canyonlands will come alive beyond your wildest dreams.

ENJOY!

DAY ONE

FLY TO SALT LAKE CITY

Booking Your Flights

- Arrive in Salt Lake City by **3PM** because you have a long drive (2.5 hours) to **Price, Utah** after the flight.
- **WHEN YOU BOOK YOUR ROUNDTRIP TICKET TO SALT LAKE CITY YOU NEED TO MAKE SURE THAT YOUR RETURN FLIGHT DOESN'T LEAVE BEFORE 6 PM SO THAT YOU HAVE TIME THAT LAST DAY TO VISIT TEMPLE SQUARE IN SALT LAKE CITY BEFORE FLYING HOME.**

Booking Your Hotels

Book **all** your rooms in advance. But make sure they allow for **free cancellation.**

The Southwest is a very popular destination in the Spring & Fall, so you should book your hotel far in advance. Most online bookings allow for **free cancellation** up to a few days before your arrival, so there is no down-side to booking as early as you can. If you wait, then you will probably find that there are limited rooms available. **BOOK EARLY!**

How to Get There

- Get on I-80 E from Crossbar Rd and Terminal Drive (2.7 mi)
- Follow I-15 S and US-6 E to W 100 N/W 1st N St in Price. Take exit 240 (Spanish Fork) from US-6 E (120 mi)
- Stay on W 100 N/W 1st N St. Drive to E Main St in Price, Utah (1.1 mi)

Where to Stay

- **Super 8** in Price, Utah (Indoor Pool) ***https://www.wyndhamhotels.com/super-8/price-utah/super-8-price/overview?CID=LC:SE::GGL:RIO:National:07207&iata=00065402***
- You will find all the chain motels in Price. It's a big regional town. So, you should be able to easily book a room online.

Camping

- **El Rancho Motel** & RV Campground in Price ***https://mapcarta.com/23423310***
- Your best option for **FREE!** Primitive camping is going to be a bit tricky because Price is a pretty big town and it will take some work to get to the nearest BLM land. Take the **South Carbon Avenue** exit (UT 10) off US 191. Go a short distance and take a right on **Byproducts Road**. Take your first right onto **South Fairgrounds Road** which will parallel US 191 in the direction (north) you previously came. Go a mile or so and when the road starts to make a big sweeping turn to the left, go straight onto **W 250 S**. Go another mile and start looking for a gravel road on the right or the left side of the road. To be honest, I would just camp at the El Rancho Motel & RV Campground and avoid dealing with the hassle of finding a BLM camping spot in such an active area, especially after a long flight and drive.
- **You can primitive camp anywhere you like for up to 14 days in any national forest in America for free unless it is clearly posted that you can't. It is the same for all Bureau of Land Management Lands (BLM). And most of the lands you will be passing through are either National Forest or BLM. BUT, not Park Service lands! You must always camp in a campground or obtain a backcountry camping permit to camp in a National Park.**

Where to Eat

- Dinner - **Cubby's** in Spanish Fork, Utah. Convenient stop a few miles after you exit I-15 on the right side of Highway 6. Informal dining spot that is very popular with the locals, featuring Chicago beef specialties and great salads. This is about the halfway point of your drive. ***http://cubbyschicagobeef.blogspot.com/p/menu.html***

Best Things to Do

- You have a pretty long drive ahead of you (2.5 hours) after getting off the plane, so you want to avoid a lot of stops on your way to Price. Basically, you will break the drive-in half by stopping to eat in Spanish Fork and then push on to Price. After a grueling flight and drive, you need to get to Price as early as possible (preferably in the daylight) so you can rest, get a good night's sleep, and be ready to go the next day. So, while there are some very interesting sights along the way, snap a few photos and just keep driving.

Alcohol Laws in Utah

- The alcohol laws in Utah are some of the most restrictive in the United States. A person must be 21 years old to buy or consume alcohol. Current Utah law sets a limit of 3.2 percent alcohol for beer sold at grocery and convenience stores and at establishments operating under a "beer only" type license, such as taverns, beer bars and some restaurants, which means totally different beers masquerading in familiar cans. Beer over 3.2 percent is available in **State Liquor Stores and Package Agencies** (they tend to only be open between 10-5 and are hard to find), and at clubs and restaurants licensed to sell liquor. In commercial facilities, the time at which alcohol may be served is limited, and alcohol may not be sold any later than 1 AM under any circumstance. Unless you are doing the 14-day trip in this book, you will always be in Utah. So, when you see a State Liquor Store (Salt Lake, Vernal, Duchesne, Price, and Moab) that's where you should buy your liquor.

- **After Moab, there are no more State Liquor Stores and it's all 3.2% beer**

Hiking Rules and Tricks

- When packing for the trip, **less is better**. You can always buy something you forgot to bring when you get there. And this will reduce the weight of your luggage.
- When camping, a **large duffel** (like LL Bean's Rolling Adventure Duffel) is best for carrying all your car camping gear and clothes in one bag, thus avoiding multiple bags.
- Keep your food in your car. Animals can smell it a mile away - especially rodents and bears.
- I never bring pots and pans or even start a fire when I am camping (I do carry a lighter in case of an emergency.). Fires are dangerous in a windy place like the Southwest and should be avoided. Plus, it will slow you down in the morning, having to make sure your fire is completely extinguished. Camp stoves and fuel are also a needless headache. **Eat a big dinner after your last hike of the day**. And then snack at your camp. If you are one of those people who need some coffee in the morning, get it on the road or put some in a thermos the night before. If you are staying in a developed campground, fires are lots of fun and a big part of the whole camping experience. So, fire away!
- CAUTION! Rocks occasionally fall on most hiking trails. If you see an active rockfall, immediately leave the area.
- Horses have the right-of-way. Stand on the uphill side of the trail to let the horses pass. Don't make any loud noises or wild gestures, and please give them warning of your presence.
- Pack out all trash, including tissue paper and cigarette butts.
- To avoid environmental impact, bring a reusable water bottle. Every park provides water filling stations. Our parks are being trashed by those stupid "spring water" plastic bottles. Most of the time the water is from a municipal water source, not some

fresh crystal spring. In fact, the water at the parks is undoubtedly cleaner and better tasting.

- It is a federal crime to remove **ANYTHING** from a natural park – a piece of pottery, a rock, a flower, or even a leaf. Imagine if everyone who visited a national park just picked up one thing and took it home. Over time, the place would be diminished for all future generations to come. So, look, but leave it alone.
- Do not throw anything, anywhere, at any time!
- Be respectful of others; keep noise levels down. Talk, don't shout.
- Stay on maintained trails. Please do not take shortcuts because it causes erosion and will eventually wash out the main trail.
- Uphill hikers have the right-of-way unless they stop and then signal you to come ahead.
- Do not feed the wildlife. It can be very tempting. They are very cute little beggars. But feeding them changes their dietary habits and eventually weans them from natural foods. Animals that beg are invariably thin and emaciated because their diet consists of M&M's and other junk food that is not nutritious.
- The biggest safety threat from animals are not bears, scorpions, snakes, or mountain lions. More people die in our national parks from **bee stings** than from any other animal. Bees in Canyon Country can be very aggressive, especially around food. If you know that you are allergic to bees, you should carry an Epi Pen in case you are stung and go into anaphylactic shock.
- Remember: You are entering a wild setting. Ultimately, you are responsible for your own safety, and the safety of those around you.
- If you take a dirt road and come to an unlocked gate, make sure you close it. Ranchers graze their cattle throughout the high desert and if you leave the gate open the cows will escape. And this will spell **BIG** trouble for you.

Insider Tips

- **Make sure that your vehicle comes equipped with GPS**. If you must pay extra, so be it, because it's worth having that very valuable assistance. For the times when you don't have an internet connection, you can use this guide book. And be sure to stop at the visitor centers in each town and park and pick up a **FREE!** paper state highway map.
- Here's a very valuable mapping trick to get around the times when you do not have an internet connection, using Price, Utah and Arches National Park as an example. When you get up in the morning at your hotel in Price, you will have a good internet connection. Open google maps. Type in "Arches National Park" and that area will appear on your phone. Just leave it there for future use when you are at the park later in the day. When you get to Arches you definitely will **not** have any internet, but when you open the google map that you previously downloaded it will still provide you with the "little blue dot" function that will follow you as you move even though you are not connected to the internet. How can that be, you ask? Because the phone is using **GPS satellite tracking** and not the internet. Yes, it's like magic. And you can use this little trick wherever you go. I use it all the time in Europe where I never have an internet connection other than in Wi-Fi cafes.
- Take advantage of **FREE!** Map apps for your phone or iPad that will put some outstanding maps at the touch of your finger.
- Don't be afraid to talk to the locals. They know the latest and the greatest. Most folks you will encounter are incredibly friendly and would be happy to steer you in the right direction.
- Most restaurants in Utah's small Mormon towns close by **9PM**.
- Watch your speed when driving through any town because the police enforce the speed limit with great gusto!
- **Almost every place or service mentioned in this guide book has its own website that can provide additional information, up-to-date costs, and maps.**

Save Money!

- Stop at Walmart Supercenter and Discount Liquors in Price, Utah and it will save you money buying your essential supplies for the trip.
- **Annual Pass** - Purchase an Annual Pass when you enter Arches National Park, which will save you $20 in the long run because you won't have to pay $25 every time you enter another national park or monument during the trip (there will be 5). The pass costs $80 and is good in any National Park, National Monument, or National Recreation Area in the country for a whole year.
  https://www.nps.gov/planyourvisit/passes.htm
- **Senior Pass** - If you are a US citizen or resident and 62 years or older you can get the best deal in recreation. A Senior Pass costs only $80 + $10 handling fee for a lifetime pass. It enables free admission for your entire carload to National Parks, National Monuments, and many other fee areas managed by other federal agencies.
  https://www.nps.gov/planyourvisit/senior-pass-changes.htm
- **You can purchase your Annual or Senior Pass at the entrance station to the first national park you visit,** rather than go through the hassle of purchasing it online or through the mail. The price is the same!
- Many of the Mormon towns stage local fairs and special events that are **FREE!** So, check at the Visitor Centers to see what's happening as you are passing through.
- Download one of the many **FREE**! Star chart apps onto your cell phone so you can use it to see what you are looking at in the night sky. This is a great way to learn the constellations.
- Full moons, sunrise, sunset, and stargazing are **FREE**! And there is no better place on earth to see the stars than Canyonlands. The **International Dark-Sky Association** works to protect the night skies for present and future generations, and they

produce a map each year showing **light pollution zones** around the globe. They also designate **"Dark-Sky Parks"**, of which Canyonlands is one. So, stargazing in southeastern Utah is stellar (bad pun intended), and you should take advantage of it almost every night by driving out into the high desert and watching the stars for a few hours while drinking a few frosty beverages.

http://www.darksky.org

DAY TWO

ARCHES NATIONAL PARK

Arches can be a very hot place in spring, summer, and fall with very little shade, so you will need to make sure that you arrive at Arches National Park by nine and drive directly to the Delicate Arch trailhead. The Park Service has expanded the trailhead parking at Delicate Arch several times over the years, but it will never be big enough and usually fills by ten, so it's best to get an early start.

Delicate Arch is Utah's most iconic natural feature. It's featured on their license plates! And it is by far the most popular destination in the park. So, you should fully expect to encounter a mob scene and a human train all along the 1.5-mile-long trail (3 miles round trip), no matter what time you hike the trail. Sunset, while undoubtedly the best time to view Delicate Arch, is crazy busy. You will feel like you are in the Army and marching in a parade. So, avoid the temptation to do the sunset hike unless you don't mind big crowds.

Upon arriving at the crowded Delicate Arch trailhead there will be tour buses and large school groups in the parking lot and many people waiting to use the bathrooms. The trash cans are often overflowing, and it has the feel of a sporting event or a rock concert.

So, get there early!

Utah is world-renowned for its many well-preserved fossils that were deposited millions of years ago in what were once ancient sea beds. This part of America and most of the Canyonlands were transformed from oceans, to lakes, to rivers and swamps many times over. Every rock formation you will pass through during your trip started

as a sand dune or the bottom of some large body of water. Then they were uplifted into their current position when the continental tectonic plates smashed into one another. Wind, water, and erosion have done the rest.

After visiting Arches National Park, you will venture into the happening town of Moab, known the world over as the mountain bike capital of the world. Moab has always marched to a different beat, first as a uranium town, the film center for Western movies, and then in the 70s as the home of the counterculture hippies. Today it resembles a commercial for Patagonia outdoor hedonism. It's essentially a red-ock playground. So, make sure you take the time to roam the streets, check out the weird mix of stores and eateries, and talk to some of the friendly locals.

There is no place in Utah quite like Moab!

How to Get There

- Drive I-70 East to the exit for US 191 South. (16.7 miles) The speed limit is 80!
- Turn right onto **US 191 South** to the Arches Entrance Road on the left which is about 4 miles east of Moab. (27 miles) ***http://www.discovermoab.com/***

Where to Stay

- **Super 8 Motel** in Moab, Utah ***https://www.wyndhamhotels.com/super-8/moab-utah/super-8-moab/overview?CID=LC:SE::GGL:RIO:National:02856&iata=00065402***
- You will find all the chain motels in Moab. It's a big regional town. So, you should be able to easily book a room online.

Camping

- There are several excellent **fee-based campgrounds on UT 128 along the Colorado River**. To avoid the hideously noisy

Canyonlands by Night, the boat and truck sound and light show that runs up the canyon at sunset, you should avoid the lower camps, like where I used to stay at **Goose Island**, and camp instead at **Big Bend Campground** which is 7 miles up-canyon. Or you can camp at **Lower** or **Upper Drinks Campground** which are just before Big Bend.
http://www.discovermoab.com/campgrounds.htm

- The Bureau of Land Management is getting much more restrictive about primitive camping around Moab, so you should stick to the **fee-based campgrounds** along the Colorado River on **UT 128**.

Where to Eat

- Breakfast - **Big Moe's** in Price, Utah
https://www.facebook.com/pages/Big-Moes-Eatery-and-Bakery/11631254505686
- Lunch - Snacks. You will be in Arches National Park from morning until late afternoon and there is no place in the park to get lunch. You might want to stop at Subway or one of the sandwich places in Green River, Utah before you leave for Arches and pack a lunch in your cooler, so you can picnic in the National Park.
- Dinner - **Zax** has the biggest beer selection in town and they serve gorgeous pizza. I know that's a weird word to use for a pizza but check it out. It really is. They offer a great all-you-can-eat pizza bar and their upstairs patio deck is an amazing place to dine.
http://www.zaxmoab.com/

Best Things to Do

- Eat breakfast and check out of your hotel in Price by **8AM**.
http://www.priceutah.net/
- After breakfast drive one block north on S 700 E and then turn right on East Main Street and look for the **Walmart Supercenter** on your left. They are open 24 hours a day!

- Buy an inexpensive cooler, a case of bottled water, drinks, snacks, camping supplies, and a cheap lawn chair for each person in your party.
- Drive to Arches National Park via Green River, Utah ***https://www.nps.gov/arch/index.htm***
- On your way into the park, stop for five minutes at the Visitor Center at the park (you will return for a longer visit at the end of the day) and pick up the **FREE!** park map. **If they give you a park map at the entrance station, then don't stop at the Visitor Center.**
- Hike to Delicate Arch. ***https://www.nps.gov/arch/planyourvisit/delicate-arch.htm***
- After your hike to Delicate Arch, drive to the **Devil's Garden** at end of the park road, a winding ribbon of asphalt that is lined with non-stop, eye-popping pinnacles and arches of red sandstone formations rising into the sky. The story of Arches is a complex tale of many chapters filled with long-extinct oceans, sand dunes, salty inland seas, coastal plains, braided river systems, and swamps. The underground salt dome created by the evaporating ocean that covered the area over 300 million years ago eventually punched its way to the surface and when it did, it cracked the sandstone above like the surface of a freshly-baked loaf of bread which then eroded into all sorts of weird ridge lines, including arches of all shapes and sizes. Stop at several of the new pullouts to soak in the beauty and take some pictures. There are also short side roads that lead to scenic overlooks and quick hikes. Arches National Park has **more arches than any place else on earth – at last count there were over 2,000**. And they are continuously finding more!
- The Devil's Garden loop trail is 7.8 miles long and takes several hours. It has a few steep grades, the sun exposure is intense, and there are some short stretches of soft sand that are not fun to walk through. And after hiking Delicate Arch you are undoubtedly going to be tired. If it's hot (which it probably will be), it's best not to toy with heat exhaustion. So, you might want

to dial it back by only hiking about a mile (2 miles round trip) out to Landscape Arch, the fifth largest arch in the world and the longest in Arches National Park. This first mile section is flat and an easy walking. Double O Arch is just a little bit farther past Landscape Arch but the trail climbs steeply up a sandstone ridge with narrow ledges and steep drop-offs with no shade. But you can still check it out from a vantage point near Landscape Arch and then call it a day. On the way back, take the short spur trails to Tunnel Arch and Pine Tree Arch.
https://www.alltrails.com/trail/us/utah/devils-garden-loop-trail-with-7-arches

- After returning to the trailhead, drive leisurely back to the park entrance, stopping at several interesting attractions you missed on our way out, like **Sand Dune Arch**, **Fiery Furnace Viewpoint, Panorama Point, Balanced Rock, and Petrified Dunes Viewpoint**.
- Spend at least an hour at the truly exceptional **Visitor Center** where they offer a very informative short film about the park's weird geology, colorful exhibits about the history of the park and Grand County, a goofy sculpture of Delicate Arch, and a huge gift shop where you can buy some neat trinkets for friends and family.
- Check into your motel and go for a swim.
- Drive to the **Moab Rock Shop** on the north end of town, whose mercurial owner, **Lin Ottinger**, was one of the heroes in **Edward Abbey's** infamous novel **"The Monkey Wrench Gang".** Inside and out, you will find an amazing assortment of mineral, gemstones, fossils, geologic maps, miners lanterns, Devil's claws, dinosaur bones, jewelry, lapidary, petrified wood, Indian pottery, old mining equipment, and indescribable works of art.
http://www.moabrockshop.com/
- Dine on one of **Zax's** lovely patios that has, like most of the outdoor dining places in town, misters to cool you down. It is the

perfect way to end your day of fun and exploration in Arches, and to begin your extended visit to trippy Moab.

- After dinner, explore the interesting and eclectic mix of stores along **Main Street**.

Best Hikes

- **Delicate Arch** - This is the premiere hike in the park. The trail runs across open slickrock with no shade. The first half-mile is a well-defined trail. Follow the rock cairns. There are some interesting stops at the beginning of the trek, like an **old homestead** where some crazy wildcat rancher once carved out a surreal existence within the rocky inferno. And there is a nice **rock art panel** tucked into an **Entrada Sandstone** wall on the left where desert-dwelling Indians carved pictures of people on horses and bighorn sheep. The trail climbs steadily (480′) and then levels off near the arch. The Park Service has recently rerouted the trail to avoid the fragile, black-crusted **cryptogamic soils** that are some of the oldest life forms on earth. **Don't walk on the crusty black soil!** You should expect to find many people sitting and standing around the rim of the white and red sandstone bowl where Delicate Arch is majestically perched. Hikers wait patiently in line to get their picture snapped while standing under the massive arch. There is a shady spot to the left of the arch where you can sit and just watch the amusing parade of people. It is sort of like being in a great outdoor cathedral. People speak in whispers and even the kids are quiet and respectful. The sacred things in life are not always man made. Plan to spend about three hours hiking up and back to Delicate Arch. (3 miles round-trip - 3 hours)
- **Devil's Garden Loop Trail** - This trail will take you to **eight** of the premiere arches in the park. It is a strenuous hike along a well-maintained trail. But don't expect to be alone. This is also a very popular trail! Basically, the main trail loops around the desert with short spur trails to the arches. The first arch is **Tunnel Arch.** The second is **Pine Tree Arch**. The third, **Landscape Arch**, is a whopping 306-feet-long monster and is one of the

largest in the world. At this point you will do some climbing, first to **Wall Arch**, and then a short steep climb up to **Navajo** and **Partition Arches**. Partition Arch offers some grand, sweeping views of the high desert and is probably going to be your stopping point. But if you still haven't had enough, you can hike another 2.4 miles (roundtrip) out to **Double O Arch** and **Dark Angel Arch**. Turn around and retrace your path back to the trailhead. (7.8 miles - 5 hours)

Insider Tips

- Arches is undergoing a **multi-year construction project on the 18-mile main road** through the park that involves some widening and the installation of numerous pullouts and drainage features. They don't work on Saturdays and Sunday, so you should **plan your trip, so you are there on a weekend**. And you should check the **park website** before your trip to learn about the current conditions and if there any closures. ***https://www.nps.gov/arch/planyourvisit/conditions.htm***
- The Devil's Loop trail is crowded and some of the arches may be mobbed when you get there. Given that you will be retracing your route, you can just keep walking and stop at the arch on your way back, with the hopes that it won't be so busy.
- You can't swing a cat in Moab without hitting a pretty good restaurant. The best restaurants on websites like TripAdvisor will steer you to the places that are super expensive and fancy-schmancy. But here's what you do when you don't know where to eat: **ask a local**. It works well every time. And it's fun to talk to the people who live in the town you are visiting. You will invariably learn a lot and make new friends.
- There are several good groceries along Main Street (south side of town) and you will want to stock up on snacks and other items like fresh fruit that you can put in your cooler for the days when there is no place to eat lunch. The City Market is your best bet for the best prices and widest selection. ***https://www.citymarket.com/stores/details/620/00410?cid=loc62000410_gmb***

- There is a State Liquor Store and you will want to stop in and stock up on real booze for your stay. Remember that the beer in the groceries is only 3.2%. ***https://abc.utah.gov/stores/index.html?storeNum=27***
- There are many good **outdoor outfitters** in Moab and it is a great place to buy or replenish your camping gear and supplies.
- The **Moab Adventure Center** on Main Street offers hummer safaris, mountain biking, tours of Arches National Park, zipline and ropes, flights and horseback rides, hot air balloon rides, jet boat tours, and jeep rentals. www.moabadventurecenter.com
- "Moab, Utah, well known for its spectacular mountain biking, also boasts some of the best road biking in the West. With the recent completion of the **Moab Canyon Pathway**, connecting Moab to two national parks and one state park, there are now over one hundred miles of paved non-motorized trails through amazing scenery. Moab Canyon pathway is not just a bike lane on the side of the highway, but a path that allows riders/users to avoid the busy four-lane Highway 191 and have safe access to the state and national parks.

  The path begins at the pedestrian/bike bridge that crosses the Colorado River on Highway 128, just north of Moab. The super smooth blacktop snakes through 2 miles of the red rock canyon to the entrance of Arches National Park where you can exit for a 30-40 mile out and back ride, depending on your route choice inside the park.

  The path continues past Arches National Park for another 6.5 miles, and 525 vertical feet of climbing, crossing under Highway 191 to the beginning of Highway 313. The options here are to turn back for a scenic and speedy return from a short training ride, or to continue riding on Highway 313 for a challenging 24-mile climb to Dead Horse Point State Park or a 35-mile ride to Grand View Point in Canyonlands National Park's Island in the Sky. These mileages on Highway 313 are one way, so, with some figuring, riders can put together amazing century rides in some of the most beautiful country in the world!

Mountain bikers and cyclocross riders will love the paved bike path as it gives direct access to the multiple trails at the **Moab Brands Trail System** (at mile 6) which adds a great warm-up on pavement to the trail and slickrock rides. From there, mountain bikers can access unlimited miles of dirt and slickrock routes including the **Sovereign Trail, Bartlett Wash and Monitor & Merrimac areas**.

Not only bike riders will love this trail, but also hikers, runners, joggers and non-motorized vehicles of all sorts. Parents can pull their babies behind their bikes in trailers and all ages can enjoy the pathway, even if it is just for a leisurely stroll. Kids can try their new bikes on the flat sections on either end, since only the middle 4 miles have noticeable grade. It also provides a great place to hone your cross-country skiing skills during the off season with roller skies.

- Future plans for more paved bike paths include the Millsite Riverside Trail and a bike lane from the city of Moab to the Colorado River pedestrian bridge."
  http://www.discovermoab.com/moab_road_biking.htm

Save Money!

- You will save a lot of money by shopping for supplies at the **Walmart Supercenter** in Price, Utah.
- Before you leave the Arches National Park Visitor Center, pick up the **FREE! maps**, especially for the areas where you will be traveling next.
- The Moab Rock Shop is **FREE!**
- Parking is **FREE!** for an unlimited amount of time around Main Street in Price, Green River, and Moab.
- Visit some of the **FREE!** Art galleries in Moab.

DAY THREE

CANYONLANDS NATIONAL PARK - ISLAND IN THE SKY

You will begin your day with a splash of pioneer and movie-making history at Moab's finest museum.

And then it's off to one of America's most enticing parks. Many of the folks who visit the Moab area stop at Arches and then move on to the other spectacular attractions in the area. Lord knows there is plenty to see. So, Canyonlands National Park is rarely very crowded, and the pace is relaxed. Canyonlands is comprised of two distinct areas, a magnificent mesa in the clouds called Island in the Sky, and a dazzling pincushion of sandstone pinnacles called The Needles.

The bad news is: You won't have time to see both sections of the park because they are separated by 120 road miles.

The good news is: You can see The Needles from a jaw-dropping viewpoint at Island in the Sky where you will be going today.

You will hike several short trails in the park, each completely different, and none of them very difficult. And you will stop at vistas that offer jaw-dropping views that seem like landscapes painted by the world's greatest grandmaster.

On your way back to Moab you will visit a grand viewpoint renowned the world over for its sensational sunsets.

And you will end your day eating dinner in Moab's only brewery where the locals go to eat and play.

So, get ready for some big fun!

How to Get There

- Drive north on US 191. (11 miles)
- Turn left onto UT 313 (15 miles)
- Continue straight on Grand View Point Road/Island in the Sky Road. (13 miles)
- Turn right on Upheaval Dome Road to the park entrance. (1.4 miles)

After checking out Canyonlands head over to Dead Horse State Park for a spectacular sunset view from the overlook:

- Backtrack the way you came into the park, heading east on Grand View Point Road. (14 miles)
- Turn right on UT 313 to Dead Horse State Park which is signed. (4 miles)

Where to Eat

- Breakfast - **Jailhouse Cafe**, housed in the town's original jail. I always stop there when I'm passing through town. It's got it all: great location, congenial staff, fast service, and yummy eats. ***https://www.tripadvisor.com/Restaurant_Review-g60724-d677318-Reviews-Jailhouse_Cafe-Moab_Utah.html***
- Lunch - Snacks. You might want to stop at Subway or one of the sandwich places in Moab before you leave for Island in the Sky and pack a lunch in your cooler, so you can picnic in Canyonlands National Park.
- Dinner - **Moab Brewery**. This is the local favorite and they brew a wide assortment of beers and IPA's. ***http://www.themoabbrewery.com/***

Best Things to Do

- Finish breakfast by **9AM**, and then it's time to check out some more of the town center, starting with the **Museum of Moab**, just a block away from the **Information Center** on Main Street. Walk up the airport runway-wide **E. Center Street**, to a small and rather bland brick museum on the right, sitting across from the stately **Grand County Office Building.**
- The **Moab Museum** is a fun and informative place to explore during the heat of the day, or after a morning hike. It's run by a charming hippie lady named **Barbara Jackson** who only charges **$5** for an experience that is priceless. Barbara has small rooms that showcase: paleontology, archaeology, geology, uranium mining, Anglo and Indian artifacts, the Civilian Conservation Corps camps in the area, adventure tourism, the Sagebrush Rebellion versus Ecodefenders, historic photos, a 1928 player piano, big cattle companies, the 1881 "Pinhook Battle" up in Castle Valley fought between the local Utes and several ranchers, the Old Spanish Trail, and the storied history of movie making in Professor Valley. Be sure to watch the captivating twenty-minute film about the actors and players who filmed many of the old Westerns around Moab. On the second floor you will find some fine Southwest photos; an outstanding assortment of polished stones in red velvet display cases; the first doctor's office run by Dr. JW Williams ($150 a year) who also sold drugs, books, stationery, Navajo baskets, wagons and buggies; and a very detailed re-creation of what the inside of a house in Moab would have looked like in the early 1900's. ***http://www.moabmuseum.org/***
- Drive to Canyonlands National Park - Island in the Sky. As always, your first stop in the **Canyonlands National Park** should be the **Visitor Center**. The one at Canyonlands is not up to snuff in relation to many other national parks, like nearby Arches, but they have a short movie that does a nice job of explaining the park's history and geology, and there is an okay gift shop. It is worth the 45-minute stop. And they have air conditioning!

https://www.nps.gov/cany/index.htm

- After the Visitor Center, begin your hiking day at the south rim where there is an excellent viewpoint overlooking **The Needles** section of the park to the south. And there is an excellent **rim trail** that begins at the Overlook and offers mega-views of the Green River. After checking out the South Rim, slowly work your way back up the main road, doing several short hikes in different landscapes, thus getting a good cross-section of this magnificent park. (see best hikes below)
- On your way back from the park make a 4-mile detour to **Dead Horse Point State Park** where you can catch an amazing **sunset. Check the precise time for sunset at the Canyonland National Park Service Visitor Center, so you can be right on time, along with many other sun worshipers**. The park is open year-round from 6 a.m. - 10 p.m. There is a **$15** entrance fee that is good for three days. The main viewpoint can be reached by car and is wheelchair accessible. They offer 8 miles of hiking trails and 17 miles of mountain bike trails that lead to spectacular overlooks. And they have a 21-unit campground that is open all year with electricity, a sanitary disposal station, and nice restrooms. They also have yurts to rent by reservation. This is a very popular place to watch the sun go down while the Canyonlands and the **horseshoe bend in the Colorado River** turns neon red. And there is, of course, a legend surrounding the place. In the 1800s, cowboys used to catch wild horses by driving the stallions and their mares toward the edge of the cliff and then use the 30-yard-wide point as a horse trap. The narrow neck of the rim was a natural corral. According to the legend, a band of horses were left corralled at the end of the dry point where they died of thirst within view of the Colorado River 2,000 feet below. This is also the spot where **Thelma and Louise** jumped their blue 1966 Thunderbird. ***https://stateparks.utah.gov/parks/dead-horse/***
- Drive back to Moab and then go to dinner at the **Moab Brewery** on the south end of Main Street. The Moab Brewery is a classic local favorite. The food isn't anything special, but

they have all the Utah microbrews, including almost every IPA brewed in the West. This is where the Moabites go to eat and drink and there are very few tourons. It is a cavernous building resembling a warehouse with high ceilings from which they hang boats and bikes. They even have several tricked-out jeeps with dummy drivers scattered around the dining tables. It's a unique Southwest hangout and a must see when visiting crazy Moab.

- This is going to be your last night in Moab and if you are still looking for some entertainment you can check out some live country/western/rock music at the **Blu Pig** which is the **only place in town offering live music seven days a week**. ***http://www.blupigbbq.com/***
- If you are too tired to party after yet another action-packed day, then just head back to the hotel and sit in the hot tub, drinking boat drinks and watching the star show on the sky tube instead. A person can only have so much fun.

Best Hikes

- There are quite a few good hikes in Island in the Sky, but you will not have time to do them all. And some of them are strenuous and quite difficult. **As always, your first stop should be at the Visitor Center**. I would recommend that you begin your hiking day at the south end of the park. There is an excellent viewpoint where you can see The Needles section of the park in the distance. There is an exhilarating rim trail that begins at the Overlook and will offer views of the Green River. After checking out the South Rim, you can work your way back, explore different areas by doing several short hikes, thus getting a good cross-section of this magnificent park. The park trails are works of art, some of the finest in America, and undoubtedly the work of a real artisan. They have these huge sandstone block cairns and beautiful chiseled steps through the slickrock. The trails in this park are exceptional! ***https://www.nps.gov/cany/planyourvisit/hiking.htm***

- **Grand View Point** - Easy walking along the canyon edge to the end of Island in the Sky Mesa with panoramic views. Below the rim, you can see segments of the 100-mile **White Rim Road** looping around and below the Island in the Sky mesa top. Four-wheel-drive trips usually take two to three days, and mountain bike trips take three to four days. When the weather is dry, the White Rim Road is moderately difficult for high-clearance, four-wheel-drive vehicles. The steep, exposed sections of the **Shafer Trail, Lathrop Canyon Road, Murphy's Hogback, Hardscrabble Hill, and the Mineral Bottom** switchbacks make the White Rim loop a challenging mountain bike ride and require extreme caution for both vehicles and bikes during periods of bad weather. From your lofty perch in the sky, a lone jeep creeping slowly along the tiny buff ribbon of dirt road below looks like the Mars Rover. (2 miles - 1.5 hours)
- **Mesa Arch** - Easy walk to the arch at the edge of the canyon. Great place to snap a photo. Check out the interpretive sign about fragile soils. And then notice the area around the sign and see how numerous hikers have ignored the warning and destroyed a thousand years of soil by their careless steps. (0.5 miles - 30 minutes)
- **White Rim Overlook** - Walk to an east-facing overlook for some breathtaking views of the Colorado River, Monument Basin, and the La Sal Mountains. Limited trailhead parking. (1.8 miles - 1.5 hours)
- **Whale Rock** - Short but somewhat steep walk up Whale Rock leads to views of Upheaval Dome and surrounding area. (1 mile - 1 hour)

Insider Tips

- Along meandering Mill Creek in downtown Moab there is a lovely paved **greenway trail** lined by shady cottonwood trees that leads you past **Swanny City Park** where the **Farmers Market** is held on Fridays from 4-7.

- If there is one common denominator to the national parks in the Southwest, it is the **road construction**. The summer season is when they improve the roads, so no matter where you go, you should pretty much count on doing the "one lane ahead" dance which involves sitting in a long line of RV's and buses waiting for a pilot car to slowly come along and lead you through the work area. So, check the websites at each park to see if there is road construction. If there is, then you need to allow yourself some extra time for travel.
  https://www.nps.gov/cany/planyourvisit/road-conditions.htm
- The National Park Service will have the precise time for sunset posted in the Visitor Center at Canyonlands.
- **Trails:** Trails are marked with cairns (small rock piles). Please do not disturb cairns or build new ones. Signs are located at trailheads and intersections. All backcountry trails are primitive and rough. Water may be found in some canyons but is rarely available in others. All water should be purified before drinking. Spring and fall are the preferred times of year for hiking due to temperature and water availability.
- **Day Use Permits:** Traveling on four wheel-drive roads into Salt Creek, Horse and Lavender canyons by vehicle, bicycle or horse requires a day use permit. (See other side for permit information.)
- **Backcountry Permits:** All overnight stays, except those at Squaw Flat Campground, require a backcountry permit. Visitors are responsible for knowing and following backcountry regulations. (See other side for permit information.)
- **Pets:** Pets are only permitted on paved and two- wheel-drive roads. Pets are not allowed on trails or four-wheel drive roads (either inside or outside of a vehicle). Pets are permitted in your campsite at Squaw Flat Campground. Pets must be leashed at all times.
- **Cryptobiotic Soil Crusts:** An important feature of the Colorado Plateau is the black. knobby crust often seen growing on soil

surfaces. Cryptobiotic soil holds moisture, prevents erosion and contributes nutrients to the desert environment. The crust is easily broken and crushed by tracks. Please do not step or drive on these living soils.

Safety Information: The high desert is a land of extremes. For a safe and enjoyable visit, please follow these guidelines:

- Drink a minimum of one gallon of water per day. Avoid overexposure to the intense sun.
- Spring, summer and fall temperatures may become extremely hot. Save strenuous activity for morning or evening hours.
- During winter, temperatures drop well below freezing. Wear warm wool or synthetic clothing. Carry storm gear and a flashlight.
- During lightning storms avoid lone trees, cliff edges and high ridges. Return to your vehicle if possible.
- Watch weather conditions. Slickrock lives up to its name when wet or icy!
- Remember that climbing up is easier than climbing down.
- Flash floods occur with amazing rapidity. When caught in flash flood conditions, go to high ground. Do not attempt to drive through washes in flood.
- Group members should stay together to avoid becoming lost.
- If you become lost, stay where you are. Make your location obvious to searchers.

Save Money!

- Before you leave the Canyonlands National Park Visitor Center, pick up the **FREE! park maps**, especially for the areas where you will be traveling next.
- Birdwatching is **FREE!** And the Canyonlands is packed with many interesting and colorful birds.

- While you are at the Visitor Center in Moab, ask about the **Free! Jurassic Walks and Talks**, where you can join a BLM paleontologist and explore the world of dinosaurs. Every weekend, through the summer, a BLM dinosaur expert will lead tours of dinosaur fossils and track sites in the Moab Area, beginning at the **Moab Information Center** on Main Street. ***https://www.blm.gov/press-release/blm-invites-public-free-jurassic-walks-and-talks-near-moab-utah***

DAY FOUR

NATURAL BRIDGES NATIONAL MONUMENT

This is going to be a very busy day, packed with some wonderful attractions and loaded with Mormon pioneer history and fascinating Indian prehistory.

You will travel through a realm of glorious redrock and cedar trees that has the distinction of having the highest concentration of Indian ruins in the whole Southwest, before stopping at an amazing National Park crowned with spectacular natural bridges where you will do a fun hike framed by the controversial Bears Ears.

You will end your day cruising by several surreal sandstone monoliths on your way past the ghost village of Hite that has been marooned by the receding waters of Lake Powell.

And finally, you will land at a freaky crossroads town in the absolute middle of nowhere.

So, buckle up and let's get cracking because this is going to be a long and fun filled day!

How to Get There

- Drive US 191 South to Blanding. (75 miles)
- Turn right onto UT 95 South. (30 miles)
- Turn right onto UT 275 North to the Natural Bridges Visitor Center. (4.5 miles)

After visiting Natural Bridges:

- Backtrack the way you came into the park and turn right on UT 95 North to the Hite Overlook which is signed. (55 miles)
- Stay on UT 95 North to Hanksville, Utah.
- UT 95 ends in Hanksville. Go straight on UT 24 into Hanksville. (42 miles)

Where to Stay

- **Whispering Sands** Motel in Hanksville, Utah
  http://www.whisperingsandsmotel.com/

Camping

- **Duke's Skickrock Grill, Campground & RV Park**
  in Hanksville, Utah
  https://www.dukesslickrock.com/
- The nearest **FREE!** Primitive camping on BLM land can be found a few miles **north** of Hanksville. Follow US 24 north until you are clearly well out of town and take one of the gravel roads heading off to the right until you find a place where you would like to camp.

Where to Eat

- Breakfast - **Peace Tree Cafe** in Moab. They stamp their sandwiches with a branded peace sign.
  http://www.peacetreecafe.com/
- Lunch - **Yak's Center Street Cafe** in Blanding, Utah
  https://www.tripadvisor.com/Restaurant_Review-g56935-d4783963-Reviews-Yak_s_Center_Street_Cafe-Blanding_Utah.html
- Dinner - **Duke's SlickRock Grill** in Hanksville, Utah. They serve some excellent IPA's and wine. Their pies are homemade. They brand their hamburger buns like cattle. And you can get your picture snapped at the bar, standing next to a life-size John "Duke" Wayne, in full cowboy regalia.

Best Things to Do

- ***Please keep in mind that you still have a two-hour drive through some of the most striking landscapes in the Southwest after you leave Natural Bridges. So, you need to be conscious of the time when you stop at the attractions listed below. You have an hour and a half drive from Moab to Blanding, with two museum stops and lunch. You have very little time to dawdle if you want to hike around Natural Bridges and drive to your hotel in Hanksville in the light of day. You will need to arrive at Natural Bridges no later than 3PM.***
- After breakfast, return to the motel and check out by **8AM.**
- Buy some **fresh organic fruit** from the friendly lady selling Colorado fruit from her pickup by the right side of the road just down the road from the Super 8.
- Pick up your snacks, ice, gas, liquor and any other supplies you will need before leaving Moab. **This is the last big town you will be in for the rest of the trip!**
- As you are driving south down US 191 toward The Needles you will come to the enchanting **Wilson Arch** (91 feet long by 46 feet high) nestled in a cliff face to the left of the highway. Stop at the wide pull out and check out the impressive rock window from the side of the road and then push on.
- According to the highway sign, "Wilson Arch was named after Joe Wilson, a local pioneer who had a cabin nearby in Dry Valley. This formation is known as Entrada Sandstone. Over time superficial cracks, joints, and folds of these layers were saturated with water. Ice formed in the fissures, melted under extreme desert heat, and winds cleaned out the loose particles. A series of free-standing fins remained. Wind and water attacked these fins until, in some, cementing material gave way and chunks of rock tumbled out. Many damaged fins collapsed

like the one to the right of Wilson Arch. Others, with the right degree of hardness survived despite their missing middles like Wilson Arch."
https://en.wikipedia.org/wiki/Wilson_Arch

- Stop for about thirty minutes at the **Monticello Visitor Center** which is in the middle of town off Main Street (US 191). Attached to the center is the **FREE! Frontier Museum** where they showcase a very curious mix, starting with the standard private collections of **looted Indian artifacts** from Anasazi sites in the area, with the names of the pot hunters, like **Nell Dalton**, proudly displayed like generous benefactors; items like linens and dishes from the long-gone **Hyland Hotel**; a wooden chair from the **Home of Truth Chapel**; minerals, fossils, and monstrous **sharks teeth**; a **Champion Cowboy saddle**; a galvanized steel **ballot box**; **Ray Jarvis'** old tool collection; landline telephones and the town's first switchboard; a white oven/stove and **gas iron**; a **huge typewriter**; old dresses and a baby carriage; an **electric mangler** and all things cowboy; historic photos of cowboys and Indians; a very odd **doll collection**; medical equipment, including a **weird EKG machine**; a collection of **barbed wire**; cameras, radios, and a hodgepodge mix of unrelated items from local houses and businesses. One of the more interesting items in the Frontier Museum was the **Bull Durham Tobacco Quilt** that was made from old Bull Durham sacks by a local lady who collected them along the side of the road and from the local cowboys who saved their sacks for her too. When she had collected enough, she dyed them yellow and pink and made two lovely quilts. The quilter was following the pioneer creed: "Use It Up, Wear It Out, Make Do Or Do Without". But the strangest exhibit were items donated by the family of **Marie Ogden** of New Jersey, who came to San Juan County in 1933 after the death of her husband, with a group of about thirty followers who called themselves **The Home of Truth**. They were mostly disillusioned easterners who were fleeing the Great Depression and they were following Marie who had promised to lead them to the place of the Second

Coming of Jesús Christ. Marie's followers believed she was the reincarnation of the Virgin Mary. Apparently, the local Mormons did not find these religious fanatics amusing and no one would sell them land around Monticello. But Marie was tenacious, and she built her mission by a creek near what is today the entrance to The Needles section of Canyonlands National Park. And then she bought the "San Juan Record" newspaper in 1934 and served as its editor until 1949 when she sold the paper. She also tried her hand at farming, mining, construction projects, and taught music. She died in a nursing home in **Blanding, Utah** in 1975, at the age of 91.
http://utahsadventurefamily.comfrontier-museum-in-monticello/

- It will only take you about thirty minutes to check out the museum, and after that, spend a little time chatting with the local ladies who run the Visitor Center. They have some great stories! And the neatest thing in the whole place is **"Little Town"**, an amazing **diorama of Monticello between 1888-1911**.
- Walk outside to the adjacent barn next to the Visitor Center where you will find the ginormous 20-feet-long by ten-feet-wide by eleven-feet-high, 650 rpm, 22,725-pound, 4-cylinder gas tractor called the "**Big Four "30" – The Giant Horse"** made in 1913 by the **Emerson-Brantingham Company of Minneapolis**. It is a remnant of olden days when colossus machinery ruled the day. The initial cost of this behemoth that moved along at a top speed of 3 mph and needed a full-time maintenance crew, was $4,000, a hefty price indeed in those days for a little farming town in the middle of nowhere. But the local working wage per day was $11.20, and the total cost for using the Big Four tractor in grubbing and plowing was $3.51. So, it was a good deal – at least for a few years, until it started regularly breaking down. Eventually, they just dug a big hole out in the desert and buried the monstrosity.
- Eat a quick lunch in Blanding, Utah.

- Drive to the **Edge of the Cedars** in Blanding, Utah. This is one of the best **Indian museums** in the world and it's worth spending at least two hours at this amazing place. The Edge is a scientific museum created and curated by reputable archaeologists who have gathered the museum's artifacts through painstaking and meticulous excavations, not display cases filled with locally looted items without provenance that you find in all the little Utah museums. You see, if you don't know exactly where an artifact came from - and I mean the exact layer of dirt where it was unearthed from - then all you have is a shiny thing. It's useless from a scientific standpoint, though on the black market, it might be worth a pretty penny.

  The Edge of the Cedars Museum is the real deal, complete with excellent storyboards that explain what you are looking at and what it all really means. That said, the archaeologists are still playing the "we used to think but now we know" game about many controversial Anasazi mysteries, like what the rock art symbols mean, and why the Anasazi completely abandoned their spectacular cities like **Chaco Canyon** and **Mesa Verde** by **1300**. I still think it was a combination of factors: prolonged drought and the water table dropping, thus making it hard to farm near their homes; depletion of natural resources like wood, forcing them to go further and further afield; competition and warfare; and disease and poor nutrition. All these factors - and probably some others we don't know about - created the Perfect Storm.

  And then there's the raging **Ancestral Puebloans controversy**. The experts can't even agree what the hell to call the ancient Indians who inhabited the American Southwest. On one side we have the old school archaeologists and anthropologists who have always used the term **Native-American**. In the 70s, that term went out of vogue and everyone started calling them ***Anasazi***, a term coined by the infamous cowboy pothunter **Richard Wetherill** in the 1880s, which is a Navajo word meaning **"ancient ancestor"** or **"ancient enemy"**, depending on who you talk to. And now, in the **Political Correctness Period**, the experts have coined the tongue-twisting phrase ***Ancestral Puebloans*** because each Pueblo group has their own name. For instance, the **Hopi** refer to their ancestors as the ***Hisatsinom***. But the Acoma, Cochita, Isleta, Jemez, Laguna, Nambe, Okhay, Picuris, Sandia, Santa Ana, Santa Clara, San Felipe, Taos, Zia, and Zuni have their own names for their ancestors and don't want to use a Hopi word. In the end, we are all immigrants. The ***Indians of America*** came across the land bridge from Siberia while others perhaps came by sea. They are not **indigenous people** (a truly ridiculous phrase concocted by pinhead academics trying to sound smart) or **Native-Americans**. DNA research has proven beyond a reasonable shadow of a doubt that we are ALL Africans. But the name African-Americans has already been taken for another race of people. ***Indians*** - a name coined by Columbus who thought he had landed in India when he came ashore in the Caribbean and encountered people living there - is clearly a stupid name. America obviously has nothing to do with India. But it's as good, or as dumb, a name as any. And the many Indians who have befriended me over the years don't care about the term one way or the other. They define themselves by their **tribe**.

The museum also tries to tackle the thorny issue of locals from the Blanding area systematically looting Anasazi sites for the past century. They unravel two very intriguing CSI stories of forensic investigation. The first involving a fellow who was cleverly captured by running a DNA test on the filter from a cigarette he had tossed in the backfill from a site he was looting called **House Rock Ruin**. The looter was prosecuted under the **Archaeological Resource Protection Act of 1979**. In the second case another looter was caught and convicted because of his habit of leaving his empty Mountain Dew cans; and once again, his DNA ultimately did him in. **It is estimated that 80 percent of Indian archaeological sites in America have been looted and more than 90 percent around Blanding.**

* Check out my mystery novel "Anasazi Strip" to get a flavor for the pothunting of Anasazi sites on the Colorado Plateau.

The museum also features one of the largest pottery collections in the world, along with baskets, ornaments, jewelry, blankets and clothing, ceremonial objects, architecture and masonry styles, weapons and hunting snares, toys and dolls, and miniature pottery items that were probably made by or for children.

The **Puebloan Pathways** exhibits are organized by time period, starting with the first American Indians, called **Paleo-Indians**, who followed the land bridge from Siberia after the last Ice Age.

This is called the **Archaic Period** and began 11,000 years ago. (6500 BC - 1200 BC)

The **Basketmaker II Period** ran from 1200 BC - 500 AD

The **Basketmaker III Period** ran from 500 AD - 750 AD

The **Puebloan I Period** ran from 750 AD - 900 AD

The **Puebloan II Period** ran from 900 AD - 1100 AD

The **Puebloan III Period** ran from 1100 AD - 1300 AD

The **Pueblo Historic Period** ran from 1600 - 1959

The museum also has some amazing **photos of Canyon Country**, taken by famous Southwest photographers.

There is a fantastic exhibit featuring items that were found at the 850 AD **pueblo site** that was excavated where the Edge of the Cedars Museum is located today. This was the genesis for the creation of the museum. And the **Richards Perkins Collection** of ceremonial and utilitarian pottery in their black display cases is one of the best you will ever see.

- After viewing the inside exhibits walk back outside through the doors at the rear of the building to check out the restored **Pueblo**. They even have a sturdy wooden ladder that you can use to climb down into the restored **ceremonial Kiva**. There is also a very cool **sculpture garden** with a dancing flutist sporting a very prodigious prick. And there is a dreamy **sun sculpture** designed to pinpoint the winter and summer solstice.
- After roaming around the Kiva and sculpture garden, go back inside and peruse the extensive **Museum Store** with

its excellent selection of books; jewelry; t-shirts; and Native-American crafts, like healing balms made from native plants and **Tewa Tees prayer flags**.

- One of the neatest things about this isolated and forgotten part of Utah is that many of the businesses are now staffed by Indians.
  https://stateparks.utah.gov/parks/edge-of-the-cedars/
- Drive across **Cedar Mesa**. This land of pinyon-juniper and spacey slickrock canyons has the **highest concentration of Anasazi ruins in the entire Southwest**. The Anasazi were everywhere around this primeval area from before the time of Christ until about 1300 AD. Why here? Because it provided everything they needed and desired within easy walking distance and was easy on the eyes. There were spacious sandstone overhangs to keep them sheltered from the weather; abundant springs and seeps; arable bottom land right below their high and dry homes; plentiful wood for fire; edible and medicinal plants in abundance; large and small game all around; and a wide variety of materials from which they could make clothing, tools, and weapons. It was not too hot and not too cold. It was just right.
  https://utah.com/monument-valley/cedar-mesa
- You will catch some great views of the **Bears Ears** as you approach Natural Bridges. The Bears Ears are the two black buttes that look sort of like giant bears ears, perched above **Natural Bridges National Monument**. They are sacred to the **Navajo, Ute, and Puebloan Indians**. According to Navajo legend, the voluptuous **Changing-Bear Maiden** was fooled by the trickster **Coyote** into marriage. Soon she started turning into a bear. The maiden's two older brothers decided to quickly change her into something else before it was too late. So, they killed her. Then they chopped off her ears and threw them away. And that's where the Bears Ears buttes came from. As with many Navajo tales, the lesson is unclear. Killing your sister doesn't really transform her into anything but dead. It's just another story of men abusing unruly women, if you ask me.

But the real controversy surrounding Bears Ears is its National Monument status. President Obama made it **America's newest National Monument** right before he left office and that seriously angered many of the locals who felt that there was already too much protected federal land, of which the Bears Ears was a longstanding part, and **WAY too many Monuments**, which come with even more restrictions prohibiting things like mining and firewood cutting. So, Trump's new Interior Secretary recommended **reducing the Monument's size**, while **maintaining the Monument status for the area surrounding the Bears Ears**. And then all hell broke loose. The locals rejoiced, and the enviros went crazy.

- After living in the Southwest for many years, I am ambivalent about the issue. To further protect the Bears Ears, which was already protected, President Obama created a **Monument** that stretched for hundreds of miles, encompassing thousands of acres of land – from **Dead Horse State Park** above Moab in the north, to **Goosenecks State Park** in the South. The rationale was to create a consistent management area encompassing a huge and diverse swath of federal lands that could be protected as **one cohesive National Monument *ecosystem***. And that's all well and good. But in a hardscrabble place inhabited by stubborn and often belligerent Mormons just trying to scratch a living from an unforgiving landscape, it smacked of arrogant overreach. The land in question is not a vacation spot for these hardworking people, it is their **home**. And while they love the Bears Ears as much as the next person and **do not oppose its designation as a National Monument**, they see no reason why the government should essentially lock down a huge part of Utah to appease a bunch of people who have no idea where the Bears Ears National Monument is even located. And to be honest, I think they're right. In the end, the expansion of the Monument under Obama was a clever way to stop the extractive industries from laying waste to the fragile landscape, and really had little or nothing to do with protecting Bears Ears. And that's a noble cause. But to expand the acreage or reduce it was really just a business squeeze play with the poor Mormons who live there caught in the middle. ***http://www.standard.net/Environment/2016/12/29/why-is-bears-ears-national-monument-controversy-obama-big-deal***

- Drive to **Natural Bridges National Monument -** Given its remote location, **Natural Bridges** is one of the most lightly visited parks in America. And that's a shame because it is a real gem. The **Visitor Center** is outstanding, and their gift shop is filled with interesting items and exhibits. The park is very user friendly. Essentially, the park features three large natural bridges that were made millions of years ago when long dried up creeks blasted them open – **versus arches which are created by intrusions of water from above**. And just for your viewing pleasure they throw in a few **Anasazi ruins**. You can just drive the **9-mile, one-way loop road** and stop at the overlooks, or you can take the short, but steep, trails to the bottom of **White Canyon** and stand under the spectacular behemoths.
- Interestingly, Sipapu Bridge has always been listed as the **fourth largest natural Bridge in the world**, measuring a gargantuan **240 feet**, but the National Park Service recently got around to accurately measuring it with a laser and discovered that it was actually only **143 feet**. Quite the error, even by Parkie standards. No matter, your two or three hours visit to Natural Bridges will make your eyes flutter and your heart sing. ***https://www.nps.gov/nabr/index.htm***
- Drive to **Fry Canyon. Sandy Johnson**, a local lady, operated a sort of hippie/cowboy lodge in **Fry Canyon** about twenty miles from Natural Bridges when I was roaming around Canyon Country back in the Eighties. I always stopped there for a tasty meal and some good conversation whenever I was passing through. She had a few rundown motel rooms and a cafe where she served good eats and sold drinks and snacks. The sage-brush flat in front of the place was adorned with weird sculptures made from castoff construction materials like pipe and machinery. There was a pool table and there were usually a few locals hanging out. It was the only place where you could get

a home cooked meal between the **San Juan Trading Post** and **Hanksville**. In its heyday, back in the Forties, it was one of the **uranium** capitals of the United States. There was a temporary town there with over **3,000 miners**, many of whom ultimately died from radiation exposure, and they **served more beer in Fry Canyon than in Salt Lake City**. It's a broiling hot and windswept place. There was no electricity and water needed to be hauled in. In winter, it was a frigid ghost town. On my most recent visit in 2017, we had camped the night before at Muley Point and hadn't eaten a cooked meal since the Twin Rocks Cafe in Bluff the day before. And after hiking around Natural Bridges we were starved. But as we approached the old oasis, it was obvious the place wasn't open. The sculptures were gone, and the front door sat open, swaying in the wind like a time port into the ***Twilight Zone***.
https://en.wikipedia.org/wiki/Fry_Canyon,_Utah

- Drive through **White Canyon** - As you drive along the **Bicentennial Highway** – the road that was vandalized at the end of Edward Abbey's classic tale "The Monkey Wrench Gang" – heading west from Natural Bridges, White Canyon, the creek that created Natural Bridges, is on your right all the way to Hite, a once booming boat launch/convenience store/marina run by the National Park Service concessionaire at the head of Lake Powell. There are numerous slot canyon hikes in White Canyon – some quite dangerous. And there are several very wild geologic monoliths, like the **Cheesebox** and **Jacob's Chair**, dotting the surreal landscape to your right. Take the time to stop and just take in the beauty and silence of this remote area of America. And snap a photo at the ***Jetsons Bridge*** over the Colorado River. Look for the airplane landing strip on the left right after the bridge. When Hite was rocking back in the eighties, there were small planes landing and taking off pretty regularly.
https://www.nps.gov/glca/planyourvisit/hite.htm
- Drive past **The Rocks Swimming Hole** - There's a spot near the confluence of the Colorado River and the Dirty Devil River where a giant wedge of Navajo Sandstone squeezes UT 95

and creates a doorway effect just before the highway does a big sweeping turn to the right. Over the years, at least three different **car commercials** have been filmed there. In 1981, on my first foray into this lonely part of the Colorado Plateau, I discovered a path by this spot that led down to the refreshingly cool waters of Lake Powell. There were a series of small islands stretching out into the lake, and I would wade and swim my way out to the end of the chain where there were shady alcoves and diving rocks. The lake was deep. I called my secret swimming hole the "diving rocks spa". When we drove by on our way to Hanksville in 2017, my treasured swimming spot had been transformed into a lake-bleached, white knobby mountain of rock with grass and bushes growing in front of it. The prolonged drought is slowly changing the face of the Southwest and even the monster dams cannot stop the baking process.

- Stop at the **Hite Overlook** - Highway 95 climbs out of the Lake Powell basin and there's an amazing overlook with a stupendous (and sad) view of the dried-up lake. Entire campgrounds where people used to swim and tie their boats are now a hundred feet up in the air and a mile from the lake. The headwaters of the lake are stagnant brown from the **Dirty Devil River** which was named by the **Powell Expedition** and is now but a trickle. And the Colorado River is a mere shadow of its finer self. Hite still is in operation, but the Park Service had to build a new concrete ramp a couple hundred yards long, so people can get their boats to the lake. There is a small convenience store/gas station during the boating season. Most people now access the upper end of Lake Foul at **Hall's Crossing** or **Bullfrog**, and Hite has the lonely feel of being the last outpost. After almost twenty years of drought in the Southwest, the brimming turquoise lakes and the azure blue skies are but a fleeting memory.

  http://www.amwest-travel.com/utah-lake-powell-hite.html

- Stop and check into your motel in **Hanksville**. The little oasis of Hanksville sits just to the north of the **Henry Mountains.** The Henry's were the **last mountain range in the lower forty-eight to be discovered** and the nearby town of Boulder was the **last**

city to get mail delivery. It's pretty much the back of beyond and about as far away from anything as you can get in America south of Alaska.
https://utah.com/henry-mountains

- There isn't a lot to see and do in Hanksville. The highway running through town serves as Main Street. There's a small **Visitor Center/Medical Clinic** combo by the intersection with **UT 24**, across from the **Hollow Mountain gas station** which is a must stop roadside attraction. There's a small grocery store on the west end of town and a post office. There are two motels. There's **Blondies** for breakfast, **Stan's Burger Shack** for lunch, and **Duke's** for dinner. Dukes also has a nice campground and rustic cabins. There is a **year-round car repair** shop about a mile out of town north on UT 24. And that's pretty much it. It's a hot dusty place to bed down on the way to **Capitol Reef**. I often called it the heart of nowhere. But in its own weird way, it seems dreamy, like a science fiction movie with a happy ending.
https://en.wikipedia.org/wiki/Hanksville,_Utah
- After dinner, go **stargazing** from right in front of your hotel room. Just set up your lawn chair in the giant gravel parking lot of the Whispering Sands and take in the sky show. There aren't a lot of lights in Hanksville so the stars are easy to spot, and you don't have to get in your car and drive out of town to see them.

Best Hikes

- You can do the individual trails at **Natural Bridges National Monument** one at a time (see below), or you can just do the Loop Trail and see tall three of the main bridges all in one continuous circuit. This is the trail I always take, but you might not want to hike so far, or might not have enough time and would prefer to do them individually.
- **Loop Trail** - The 8.6-mile (13.8 km) loop trail provides an excellent way to experience the wonders of all the Natural Bridges. The full loop passes all three bridges, but you can also take shorter loops between the bridges. Join the loop trail at any of the bridge parking areas. If you want to hike the full loop, follow

the trail up the left side of the canyon after passing Kachina Bridge to skirt the "Knickpoint" pour-off.

- **Sipapu Bridge** - This is one of the largest natural bridges in the United States (Rainbow Bridge on Lake Powell is the biggest). In Hopi mythology, a "sipapu" is a gateway through which souls may pass to the spirit world. The trail to the canyon bottom below Sipapu is the steepest in the park. A staircase and **three wooden ladders** aid in the descent. At the top of the stairway, notice the logs reaching out from the cliff wall to the large fir tree on the other side of the stairs. Early visitors to the park climbed down this tree to reach the canyon. At the base of the tree you can still see the remains of an earlier staircase. The ledge located halfway down the trail provides an excellent view of Sipapu Bridge. Please use caution around the cliff edges. The remaining portion of the trail leads down a series of switchbacks and ladders to the grove of Gambel's oak beneath Sipapu. (1.2 miles - 1 hour)
  Elevation change: 500 feet
- **Kachina Bridge** - This is a massive bridge and is considered the "youngest" of the three because of the thickness of its span. The relatively small size of its opening and its orientation make it difficult to see from the overlook. The pile of boulders under the far side of the bridge resulted from a rockfall in 1992, when approximately 4,000 tons of rock broke off the bridge. As you descend the switchbacks, notice the "Knickpoint" pour-off in Armstrong Canyon below and to your left. During floods, this spout sends a muddy red waterfall plunging into the pool below. The bridge is named for the Kachina dancers that play a central role in Hopi religious tradition. There is a bathroom at the trailhead. (1.4 miles - 1 hour)
  Elevation change: 400 feet
- **Owachomo Bridge** - The word means "rock mound" in Hopi and is named after the rock formation on top of the southeast end of the bridge. From the overlook, the twin buttes called "The Bear's Ears" (America's newest National Monument)

break the eastern horizon. The original road to Natural Bridges passed between these buttes, ending across the canyon from Owachomo Bridge at the original visitor center (which was a platform tent). The old trail still winds up the other side of the canyon but is seldom used. Notice that Tuwa Creek no longer flows under Owachomo like it did for thousands of years. The bridge's delicate form suggests that it is has eroded more quickly than the other bridges. This is the shortest and easiest of the three hikes. (0.4 miles - 30 minutes)
Elevation change: 108 feet

- **Horsecollar Ruin** - There is a short and fairly flat trail across the slickrock to an impressive overlook above the Horsecollar Ruin in the bottom of White Canyon. This is a good place to better appreciate how the Anasazi lived back in the day. (0.6 roundtrip)

Insider Tips

- While you are in **Monticello** and **Blanding**, take a few minutes to drive around some of the side streets and check out the houses. There are some very interesting brick and wood frame houses and it's always fun to see how the locals live. The Mormons, as a rule, are very tidy folk who keep their properties looking nice with flowers and well-tended yards.
- Once you leave Blanding you will not be able to get a reliable internet connection or probably even cell phone service until you end the day in Hanksville. Be sure to download Natural Bridges from Google maps before you leave the Monticello, so you have a GPS map!
- The only drinking between Blanding and Hanksville will be at Natural Bridges. You might get lucky with the store at Hite, but that can be hot or miss and involves a long detour to the lake.
- A few miles west of Natural Bridges at the junction of **UT 95, the Bicentennial Highway**, and the turnoff to **Hall's Crossing (Lake Powell)** is a popular spot used by the local police for **DUI checkpoints**. If you have an open liquor container, and that would **include an opened bottle of liquor or wine in your**

trunk, you are going to get hit with a **$75** fine. They don't take checks or credit cards. And if you can't pay, they will haul your ass to jail in Monticello. I learned this lesson the hard way back in 1992, when I came upon the road block after almost dying in the **Black Box in White Canyon**, following a killer hike.

- While the air is still clearer than any east coast sky, you can't help but notice the smoke. After almost twenty years of drought with below average rainfall in the West, our forests, parks, and brushlands have been turned into fire traps. And every summer the fire season starts earlier and lasts a bit longer. As a result, the skies that used to be so crystal blue and almost shiny, are now perpetually filtered by a smoky haze. And you don't have to be near a fire for it to affect the clarity of the sky. The prevailing winds can blow smoke into the Southwest from as far away as the Pacific Northwest or the Intermountain West, meaning a fire in a national forest in Idaho can bring a smoky haze to the Four Corners Region. And while it might not smell like smoke, it still fouls the air. Welcome to the new normal.
- There is a clean bathroom at the **Hog Springs rest area** a few miles past the Hite Overlook. It's worth the stop to see the honeycombs in the sandstone walls.

Save Money!

- The **Monticello Visitor Center and Museum** is **FREE!**

DAY FIVE

LITTLE WILD HORSE SLOT CANYON

Today you are going to explore one of the finest and most accessible *slot canyons* in the Southwest, and because it's located in the back of beyond it doesn't get thousands of people visiting it each day like so many of the national parks in the region. Plus, you must get out of your car and hike to see it. So, that also keeps the numbers down. But it is still quite popular with the people of Utah, so you should expect to see a fair number of hikers.

After your hike through Goblin Valley you will drive through an enchanting world of extremes, filled with lushly irrigated valleys, multi-colored mesas, the Caineville Buttes, and the Bentonite Badlands.

And you will end your day at one of my favorite National Parks, Capitol Reef National Park.

This will definitely be a day for the ol' memory bank.

How to Get There

- Turn onto UT 24 East by the red and white Sandstone Dome gas station in Hanksville. (19.6 miles)
- Turn left onto Temple Mt. Road. (5.2 miles)
- Turn left onto Goblin Valley Road. (6.7 miles)
- As you approach the entrance station to the state park, turn right to the trailhead. (5.3 miles)

After hiking Little Wild Horse Canyon slot canyon:

- Backtrack to UT 24 West and return to Hanksville. (36.8 miles)
- Turn right onto UT 24 West and drive to Capitol Reef National Park and Torrey, Utah. (48 miles)

Where to Stay

- **Capitol Reef Resort** in Torrey, Utah. This place has it all! A great restaurant, horseback rides, and is centrally located for everything you want to see and do. It also has reliable Wi-Fi, something that many of the hotels around Torrey do not. **They say they do**, and it's usually free, but it tends to be spotty. ***https://capitolreefresort.com/***

Camping

- **Capitol Reef National Park Campground**. This is a lovely campground with trails along the river and to the historic town of Fruita. This is one of the best National Park campgrounds in the U.S.
https://www.nps.gov/care/planyourvisit/campinga.htm
- **Wonderland RV Park** in Torrey
http://www.capitolreefrvpark.com/
- Most of the land around Torrey is either private or national park land. So, I would strongly recommend that you camp in one of the commercial campgrounds in Torrey.

Where to Eat

- Breakfast - **Blondie's Eatery & Gift** in Hanksville
https://www.tripadvisor.com/Restaurant_Review-g57006-d729545-Reviews-Blondie_s_Eatery_Gift-Hanksville_Utah.html
- Lunch - **Luna Mesa** is 19 miles east of Hanksville on the way to Capitol Reef. Simple, yet tasty Mexican fare.
https://www.tripadvisor.com/Restaurant_Review-g60758-d3738817-Reviews-Luna_Mesa_Oasis-Torrey_Utah.html
- **Stan's Burger Shack** in Hanksville, Utah
http://www.stansburgershak.com/

- Dinner - **Broken Spur Steak House** in Torrey, Utah. This place is a bit hard to find but it's a local favorite, serving good food at a reasonable price. As you crest the hill on UT24 coming into the town of Torrey, look for a sign on the right for the restaurant and a road leading up onto a hill. There are fancier restaurants in Torrey, but after a long day of hiking and driving, you are probably just going to want to check into your hotel and grab a quick bite to eat. And more importantly, it has great views from atop the hill overlooking Capitol Reef and is close to the park. That means you will have a shorter drive back into the park after dinner for the ranger talk.
  https://brokenspurinn.com/the-steakhouse/
- **La Cueva** serves large helpings of authentic Mexican food and is near your hotel. This is even closer to the park and right off the highway on the right.
  http://www.cafelacueva.com/

Best Things to Do

- You should eat breakfast and check out of your hotel by **9AM**.
- Before heading over to Goblin Valley, stop at **Hollow Mountain** for some gas, snacks, and water. The store has been carved out of the inside of a brown sandstone hill and it's like walking into a big cave. They sell a little bit of everything, including an excellent assortment of Michael Kelsey guide books, which I was amazed to discover are now in their fifth printing. His original book "Canyon Hiking Guide to the COLORADO PLATEAU" was my hiking bible for many years. My, how time flies when you're having fun.
  https://www.roadsideamerica.com/tip/1314
- Hike **Little Wild Horse Canyon slot canyon in Goblin Valley**. **Goblin Valley** is in a **state park** and on **BLM land**. The state park is noted for its hoodoos and weird balanced-rock formations and is extremely popular with the people of Utah who come from far and wide to play amidst the odd assortment of rock formations.

- Goblin Valley was in the news in 2016, when some jerk decided to push one of the precariously perched rocks off its base. And rather than own it, and just admit that he was an idiot, he claimed that he was performing a public service by knocking over the rock before it fell on some unsuspecting hiker. The authorities didn't buy his story and he went to jail and was subsequently convicted of damaging natural resources and being a jerk.
  https://stateparks.utah.gov/parks/goblin-valley/
- Back in Hanksville after your hike, stop briefly at the **Visitor Center** to check on road conditions and any alerts.
- Drive west on UT 24 and experience one of my favorite Southwest drives through the **Fremont River Valley**, the **San Rafael Swell**, and the **Caineville Mesas**. It is a starkly beautiful land of brown-stained and red-streaked battleship mesas and irrigated farmlands.
  https://en.wikipedia.org/wiki/Fremont_River_(Utah)
- Eat lunch at **Luna Mesa**. But check their website to make sure they are still in business. If they aren't, then eat lunch at **Stan's Burger Shack** in Hanksville.

  Luna Mesa is the only place to eat between Hanksville and Torrey. It's a hippie/cosmic outpost that serves home cooked Mexican food. Back in the eighties, I often stopped there on my way through the area to grab a beer and take in the goofy interior that was papered in money from all around the world. But like the Fry Canyon Lodge, businesses have a short shelf life in this part of America, given the small number of local inhabitants and the marginal tourist traffic passing through the area. Plus, the place looks a little weird, starting with the name, and that can reduce their business. So, it is always wise to check in advance to see if the place where you want to eat is still in operation. In 2017, Luna Mesa was still going strong, though under fresh management. A young couple, **Dan and Cher**, along with their new baby girl, will welcome you with open arms. They serve simple food, but it's delicious and clearly made with love.

It's like dining in someone's funky kitchen and it's definitely a **"Best of the Southwest"** kind of stop.

- After passing the entrance sign to Capitol Reef National Park, you still have a way to go. Your first stop is a few miles inside the park at the historic **Behunin Cabin** which is listed on the National Register. The one room stone house measures 13′ x 17′ and **Elijah Behunin and his wife and thirteen children** lived there in 1883 for only one year before pulling up stakes and moving up-canyon to the nearby town of **Fruita**. Man, you talk about a tough life.
https://en.wikipedia.org/wiki/Elijah_Cutler_Behunin_Cabin
- Hike the **Grand Wash Trail**. There is a sign for the trail along the highway. Pull into the roadside pullout along UT 24 by a small bridge over a dry wash of boulders in a grove of big cotton-wood trees. By hitting this trail toward the end of the day you will beat the heat and the crowds.
- Continue along UT 24, stopping at the long pull out to snap some photos of the **Capitol Dome**, a colossal white dome of Navajo Sandstone that closely resembles the **Capitol Building in Washington, D.C.**
- Head past all the attractions in the historic town of Fruita. You will check these sites out tomorrow. But **stop at the Visitor Center very briefly to see about the evening ranger talk**. If the Visitor Center is closed, look for a sign by the front door telling you when the talk will begin that evening. **Wait until tomorrow to revisit the Visitor Center, see the movie, and check out the exhibits and gift shop**.
https://www.nps.gov/care/index.htm
- Proceed north toward the town of Torrey and check into your motel.
http://www.torreyutah.com/
- Go to dinner and then head back to the park and catch the **evening ranger talk in the amphitheater by the campground and river**. The ranger talks usually begins right before dark and there is one every night.

https://www.nps.gov/care/planyourvisit/ranger-programs.htm

Best Hikes

- **Little Wild Horse Canyon** - One of the finest slot canyons in the Southwest and a flat and very easy hike. Because it is just five miles from the popular **Goblin Valley State Park**, this amazing canyon is easily explored and has narrow passages as fine as any other Southwest slot canyon. **Little Wild Horse Canyon** has become the most visited location in the **San Rafael Swell**. It will take at least three hours to see the best sections along its lower end, although the usual plan is to combine a tour with neighboring **Bell Canyon** – this is an 8-mile loop that in addition to the two narrow gorges also passes high, colorful cliffs and very interesting exposed and eroded rock. There are various places good for camping further along the access road – pleasant, free alternatives to the nearby paid site in the state park. ***http://www.americansouthwest.net/utah/san_rafael_swell/index.html***

  You do **not** want to go to **Goblin Valley State Park**. And it will cost you **$13** to get into the park. The place is usually overrun with Mormon school children and church groups, and it isn't worth the cost or the time. You have better things to see.

  As you are approaching the entrance station to the state park, look for a right hand turn onto a paved road. Take that road to the trailhead by a dry wash which is a large parking lot with a bathroom and some information signs. This parking lot fills up fast, so it is wise to get there early.

  The main narrows of Little Wild Horse Canyon can be reached after just ten minutes walking from the trailhead, though they are easily missed as the entrance is a concealed slit in the right side of the canyon.

  The first half-mile of the hike is along a wide open dry wash with the occasional cottonwood tree providing some much-needed shade. Please keep in mind that this is a very hot place and temperatures often reach **100 degrees**. Once you are in the narrows, the heat will no longer be a factor. But getting to the narrows and back can be a hot proposition.

When the canyon starts to tighten up you will need to avoid the first narrow section which is a dead end that turns into a slimy red mud bog ending in a slippery rock wall. Look for a well-worn trail to the left that leads up onto a sandstone ledge. Follow the ledge for a few hundred feet until the trail drops back down into the narrow canyon beyond the mud trap.

You are now at the intersection of **Bell Canyon** and **Little Wild Horse Canyon**. There is a very hard-to-see directional sign post on the sand bench in front of you, indicating that you should **take the canyon on the right**. **Bell is the larger, main canyon to the left**.

Once you enter Little Wild Horse Canyon the narrows begin almost immediately and run pretty much continuously for the next two miles. It is slow going but there is nothing too difficult or challenging. Just take your time and stop frequently to enjoy the amazing spectacle of one of the Southwest's premier **slot canyons**.

The first time I hiked the isolated canyon, back in the early eighties, I had the place completely to myself. Little Wild Horse had yet to be discovered. But now it's on everyone's bucket list, so there will probably be lots of hikers – mostly smiling Mormon families with small children. And given how narrow the trail is, you will often have to stop periodically to let people coming back down the canyon pass by because there isn't enough room for more than one person at a time.

Little Wild Horse is so narrow that in some places the walls of the canyon come together and there is no ground to stand on. So, you must walk sideways on the canyon walls. The smooth rock faces are polished and fluted like magnificent sculptures that would put any man-made piece of art to shame. The scale is immense and the colors psychedelic.

- At the two miles mark the canyon opens up for a quarter mile and then comes to a large stagnant pool. This is as far as you will be going. You can hike up the canyon a few more miles to where it intersects with Bell Canyon, and then turn left and hike back to where you started. But once the narrows end, the rest of the trail is wide open and often dangerously hot. So, stop at the end of the narrow section, eat a snack and drink some water, and relax before heading back down canyon to the trailhead. Take your time and enjoy your second trip through the narrows because you are never going to see anything like them again in your life. And the hike back is never as fun as going up because there is no sense of exploration. But novelty is a relative term in a place like Little Wild Horse. It is an absolutely magical place. (4 miles - 3 hrs)
  http://www.americansouthwest.net/slot_canyons/little_wild_horse_canyon/
- This **Grand Wash Trail** - This is an up and back hike like Little Wild Horse, in a narrow and deep canyon, but that is where the similarities end. Hike up the deep narrow canyon a little over two miles, to the trailhead at the head of the canyon off the **Scenic Drive**, and then turn around and walk back to your car, a 4.5-mile amble through a world of eroding **Jurassic** rock encompassing **200 million years** of watery upheaval. **Grand Wash** is one of the most popular trails in Capitol Reef, so you should expect to see other hikers, especially in the upper end. The canyon follows the meander bends of the powerful river that originally carved the canyon and as the sun moves across the sky, you will find lots of shade along one side of the canyon or the other. When the sun hits the black iron streaks of **desert varnish** on the white **Navajo Sandstone** walls they look like the surreal images in a **Juan Miro** painting. In some places the **Kayenta Sandstone** walls are honeycombed with weird **waterpockets** that look like big ice cream scoops have been spooned out of the red rock. It is like geology gone mad. Keep your eyes peeled for **desert bighorn sheep** that often stand defiantly on the precarious ledges above like silent sentinels.

As you get closer to the trailhead at the head of the canyon you will undoubtedly start seeing and hearing more hikers. The hike back down-canyon is always a bit anticlimactic. But all in all, your three-hour cruise through Grand Wash will be a pure delight.

https://utah.com/hiking/capitol-reef-national-park/grand-wash

Insider Tips

- If you continue past the trailhead for Little Wild Horse, it will eventually take you all the way to I-70. But the road is unpaved, and the surface deteriorates somewhat as it follows a stony streambed. The road eventually meets Muddy Creek, the main river in the southern Swell, just downstream of its lengthy narrows section ('**The Chute**'). There are many good campsites in this area.
- You are probably wondering: **What's the difference between a slot canyon and a narrows?** Well, as I learned during the evening ranger talk entitled "Slot Canyons" in the lovely moonlit Amphitheater at **Capitol Reef National Park**, the terms are not interchangeable. **Ranger Adam** explained to us how he had tried to research the topic and "hit a wall" because there really was no standard definition for the term. So, Adam started asking his canyoneer friends for their definition and they collectively narrowed it down to this: **a slot canyon is where you can touch both canyon walls with your arms**. Narrows can only be called slot canyons if they are really narrow. I came up with another defining factor for slot canyons: **if you are in a slot canyon when a flash flood comes barreling through, you're going to die**; whereas in a narrows, you might be able to find some high ground. As an example, Little Wild Horse is a slot canyon, and Capitol Wash is a narrows; it's pretty narrow, but it's still too wide to be called a slot canyon. The **Wingate** and **Navajo Sandstone** geologic formations are where you will find a slot canyon. Nobody has any idea how many slot canyons

there are in the Colorado Plateau, but there are more than in any place else on earth.

- Wi-Fi at a lot of places in the Torrey and the Capitol Reef area is spotty. The **Capitol Reef Resort** has reliable internet and it's **FREE!**
- The **Capitol Reef Resort** has an outstanding and cheap breakfast buffet every morning, with fresh fruit that will save you money, offering a wide selection of food.

Save Money!

- The ranger talk at Capitol Reef is **FREE!**
- Before you leave the Hanksville Visitor Center, pick up the **FREE! park maps**, especially for the areas where you will be traveling next.

DAY SIX

CAPITOL REEF NATIONAL PARK

I used to say that Capitol Reef was the hidden gem of National Parks that no one knew about. Well, the world has finally found it. The Visitor Center is like a bus station and the tour buses roll in like clockwork. The most popular trails are often packed, and while it isn't as jammed as Arches National Park, it often seems quite crowded, mainly because so many of the attractions are bunched together around Fruita and the Visitor Center. The parking lots are usually full, the trails can often resemble a parade route, and the narrow, winding roads are quite busy. So, even though you are far removed from civilization, you need to be prepared to deal with lots of happy travelers.

I don't want to come across like I'm demeaning these other park visitors. Everyone has a right to experience the wonders of nature, and I would rather they hike the canyons of the Southwest than sit on their couches watching football or Oprah. We all have the same rights when it comes to visiting our national parks. They are for everybody to enjoy in their own way if they follow the rules and treat these natural treasures and their fellow travelers with respect. But, it is just more enjoyable when you are the only one there. You feel like it's all yours.

That said, your last big day in the wild is going to be a truly wonderful experience, full of hiking, history, geology, and great food.

You will begin your morning with a delicious breakfast buffet before hitting the trail for an enchanting hike to the top of a magnificent mesa with thrilling views.

Then it's off to the historic town of Fruita where you will pick fruit in their beautiful orchards.

After that, you will visit a thousand-year-old Indian rock art panel and then learn about the rugged pioneers who settled in this watery paradise surrounded by imposing canyons.

And then you will stop by a historic farm house where they serve some of the tastiest fruit pies you have ever sampled. Who doesn't like pie?

You will then hop in your car and take the mesmerizing and extremely informative Scenic Drive into the Capitol Gorge, ending with a hike into a narrow, redrock canyon that will take your breath away.

And you will end your day lounging on the back patio of a rustic inn overlooking Capitol Reef as the sun goes down, eating tasty local delicacies.

Capitol Reef is a world of opposites working in harmony. It's technically a desert. It only gets about ten inches of rain a year. And most of the rain it does get comes in flash flood bursts. But it also has two rivers running through its heart, making it a land of extremes and overwhelming beauty.

Your last day in Canyonlands will be one that you will long remember!

How to Get There

- Drive Highway 24 East back into the park and go to the Visitor Center. (10 miles)

Where to Eat

- Breakfast - **Pioneer Kitchen at the Capitol Reef Resort**. They have a delectable breakfast buffet with a wide assortment of fruit and other tasty items for a very reasonable price.

https://www.tripadvisor.com/ShowUserReviews-g60758-d9885237-r349461710-The_Pioneer_Kitchen-Torrey_Utah.html

- Lunch - **Gifford House**. They have the best homemade fruit pies you ever tasted, plus other hot-out-of-the-oven bakery items. ***https://www.tripadvisor.com/Attraction_Review-g143017-d1503679-Reviews-Gifford_Homestead-Capitol_Reef_National_Park_Utah.html***
- Dinner - **Rim Rock Inn** in Torrey, Utah. Scrumptious local food with sweeping sunset views of Capitol Reef. ***http://www.therimrock.net/***

Best Things to Do

- Eat breakfast and get on the road by **9AM**.
- Drive back to Capitol Reef and hike the **Chimney Rock Trail** on the left side of the highway.
- Drive toward the Visitor Center and stop at **Panorama Point** on the right side of the highway for a look down into **Sulphur Creek** and **The Goosenecks**.
- Drive to the **Capitol Reef National Park Visitor Center**. The Visitor Center is quite busy and a bit cramped, but well worth the stop. Check out the bookstore which is stocked with some great natural history books and maps. And the movie "Watermarks" about the park is a must see. ***https://www.nps.gov/care/planyourvisit/hours.htm***
- Before you leave the Visitor Center, purchase the brochure entitled **"The Scenic Drive of Capitol Reef National Park - Self-Guided Driving Tour"** for **$2**. ***https://www.nps.gov/care/planyourvisit/scenicdrive.htm***
- Check out some of the roadside attractions around the **Fruita Rural Historic District**, starting with the **Jackson U-Pick orchard** where you will find yourself competing with the **wild turkeys and deer** for some ripe **apples, peaches and pears** that hang from the trees like tasty jewels and litter the ground

like sour mash. After picking a small basket of fruit, return to the front gate, weigh your fruit on a little scale and pay your **$5**. It is strictly an honor system operation.
https://www.nps.gov/care/learn/historyculture/orchard-scms.htm

- Fruita was settled by the legendary Mormon homesteader **Nels Johnson** who was part of the **San Juan Mission** team that had been sent by Brigham Young to **Bluff** on the **San Juan River**. Nels arrived in 1880 and built his one room cabin in what is now the **Chestnut Picnic Area**, near the largest cottonwood tree I have ever seen. It's called the **Mail Tree** because the mailman would put the mail in little wooden boxes that were attached to the gnarly old tree. Nels realized that his homestead, located at the confluence of the **Fremont River** and **Sulfur Creek**, was the perfect spot to grow **fruit and nut trees.** And as more settlers moved into the area, the valley bottom began blooming with orchards, many of which have survived to the present. According to the Parkies, it is one of the largest orchards in the National Park system with over **3,000 trees**!
- Continue east on Highway 24 and stop at the **petroglyph panel** where Indians have been chiseling their dreams since 600 AD. The huge parking lot is usually mobbed with buses and cars. The panel is rather disappointing (but worth about 15 minutes of your time) because the Park Service has built a new boardwalk to limit direct access to the panel. In fact, they now keep visitors so far away that you can barely make out the drawings. They even have one of those goofy round metal binoculars like they put on the tops of tall buildings, so you can view the rock art from afar. If you have binoculars, bring them along. In the old days, the Parkies let you walk right up to the panel and see the glyphs up close, but given the increased visitation and threat of vandalism, they have decided to keep everyone at a safe distance.
https://www.nps.gov/care/learn/historyculture/fremont.htm
- Head back toward the Visitor Center and make one last stop at the **Historic Fruita School,** a log cabin that is a bit strange

because they have a small audio box by the window that is continuously broadcasting the voice of the school teacher instructing her students. Peer through the small window at the bare, one room school and try to imagine the Mormon children sitting obediently at their desks, learning the alphabet and practicing addition.
https://www.nps.gov/care/learn/historyculture/fruitaschoolhouse.htm

- At this point, you can drive the fifteen miles into the town of **Torrey** to get some lunch. But that is going to burn up a lot of time. And time is precious. I suggest that you turn left at the Visitor Center and begin the **Scenic Drive**. After passing the Mail Tree and the Picnic Area on your left, look for an old farmhouse on the right. This is the historic **Gifford Homestead**, and they sell freshly-baked pies, using fruit from the local orchards. Who doesn't like pie? The historic **Gifford Homestead** features a small **frontier museum and store**. And they have an incredible selection of large and small **fruit pies** and **fresh bread**. I love their mixed fruit pie. After you have purchased your pie and a cold drink, walk outside and eat your mouthwatering pie at a picnic table in the shade of a spreading cottonwood tree in the front yard.
  https://www.nps.gov/care/learn/historyculture/gifford-homestead.htm

  After devouring your delightful pie, take the **10-mile Scenic Drive to Capitol Gorge**. You are starting at the hottest part of the day, so take it easy. Stop at all of the interpretive signs along the way where you will learn about: the rock formations; the creation of the **Waterpocket Fold**; the old **Oyler Mine** where uranium was mined from the yellowish-gray **Chinle Formation**; **Cassidy Arch** which was named after the outlaw **Butch Cassidy**, who supposedly used Capitol Reef for a hideout; the **Slickrock Divide** that is the high point between two drainage areas; **desert bighorn sheep** who were reintroduced into the park after being decimated by disease from the domestic sheep; and the oddly-shaped **hoodoos and pinnacles**. The **Scenic Drive** follows the **Capitol Gorge Spur Road**, the only road through the Waterpocket Fold until 1962. The last three miles of the road are smack dab in the bottom of the drainage and would not be a happy place in a flash flood. Make sure there are no storm clouds building in any direction before driving your rental car into a potential dead zone! But have no fear because the Parkies closely monitor the weather radar and if there is even the slightest chance of a flash flood, they will close off the area.

- At the end of the road there is a large parking area for the **Capitol Gorge Trail**. When you get out of your air-conditioned car it will probably feel like you are stepping into a blast furnace. Don't let that deter you because you will be able to find shade within the narrow gorge. And be sure to check out the excellent interpretive signs under the picnic shelter at the beginning of the trail.
- During your hike, you will see the **Pioneer Register**, where the Mormon families recorded their names on the brown canyon walls. The route you are following has been used for millennia by humans and they pecked their strange symbols onto the smooth brown canyon walls. And when the Mormon pioneers came through in the 1800s, they followed the example. Mormon pioneers tagged the walls for several hundred feet and some of the inscriptions look like they had to have been done by someone standing on a ladder because they are so high up on the rock face.
https://utah.com/hiking/capitol-reef-national-park/capitol-gorge
- Return to your motel and jump in the pool before cleaning up for dinner.
- Drive back toward the park on Highway 24 and pay a visit to one of my old haunts, the **Rim Rock Restaurant & Inn**. When I first visited Capitol Reef back in the early 80's, the Rimrock was the only place where you could get a hot meal. It was run by some crazy blond Hungarian B-movie star who had been in a lot of cheesy horror films. She was married to the horror movie

mogul **Al Adamsen** who was killed a few years back by his contractor and buried under the hot tub at his home in Death Valley. Life imitating art, I guess. The place has undergone a major face lift and is hopping on the weekends. But have no fear because the place is huge and can serve lots of people. It is worth waiting for a table on the back patio with its stunning views of Capitol Reef to the east. The dinners are amazing! Try the fresh trout and local asparagus. And they have an excellent selection of scotch. I strongly recommend a few wee drams of Balvenie. You earned them!

- After dinner, head back to the park to catch the **evening ranger talk** in Capitol Reef's moonlit amphitheater.
- Drive back to your hotel by the ethereal moonlight.

Best Hikes

- The **Chimney Rock Trail** - This very fun hike will take you to the top of a rocky promontory along the edge of the Waterpocket Fold, providing expansive views of Capitol Reef and Boulder Mountain beyond. Chimney Rock is a natural red sandstone spire, eroded out of the side of the mesa, and stands 300 feet above the road. The trail starts on the north side of Highway 24, and quickly begins to ascend the side of the mesa, following switchbacks as the slope increases. After a steep climb, hikers find themselves at the beginning of the **Mesa Loop Trail**. When you get to the top of the mesa, the trail continues across the top of the world and then winds back down into a side canyon leading back to where you started your hike at the bottom. Once at the top, **you do not want to take the rest of the trail**. There is a short path out to Chimney Rock. Stop, rest, take in the views, and snap a few photos before heading back the way you came. (3.3 miles RT)

  http://www.americansouthwest.net/utah/capitol_reef/chimney-rock-trail.html
- **The Capitol Gorge Trail** - This a short, easy up-and-back hike into a narrow gorge that follows the flat, dry streambed. Along the way you will pass petroglyphs carved by the prehistoric

Fremont Culture until about 1300 AD. The Fremont Indians farmed along the once-flowing stream and they used this route as a highway (for walkers, of course). If it's hot, and it probably will be, just hike from shady spot to shady spot for about a mile until you come to the **Pioneer Register**. The trail continues down canyon, but it's the same as the first mile. And there is a trail up a steep, rocky, and exposed incline to **The Tanks**, some less that enticing natural depressions in the sandstone that were used by the local inhabitants to capture rainwater. I really don't think this spur trail is worth the effort, but it's only about a half-mile from the bottom of the canyon to The Tanks. So, knock yourself out if you aren't too tired. Return to your car the way you came in. (2.5 miles RT) ***https://www.tripadvisor.com/Attraction_Review-g143017-d3475336-Reviews-Capitol_Gorge_Trail-Capitol_Reef_National_Park_Utah.html***

Insider Tips

- The Parkies closely monitor the weather radar and if there is even the slightest chance of a flash flood, they will close off the dangerous areas. But you should always be watching the sky for impending bad weather. And when you are hiking in a narrow canyon, take note of places where you can get to high ground if needed.

Save Money!

- You can use the link I provide to download the **Scenic Drive map** and save yourself $2.
- Before you leave the Capitol Reef National Park Visitor Center, pick up the **FREE! park maps**, especially for the areas where you will be traveling next.

DAY SEVEN

MORMON TOWNS, FISH LAKE, AND TEMPLE SQUARE

Your last day on the road is going to be primarily a wondrous travel day as you work your way back to Salt Lake City and your flight home. You will be sightseeing and driving through striking landscapes and many small Mormon towns as you work your way back to *civilization* in the Salt Lake Valley.

It's a 200-mile drive, so we are going to break up the drive by stopping at lovely vistas and storybook agricultural towns along the way.

And we are even going to throw in some majestic mountains and a lovely lake where you can get out and stretch your legs for good measure.

You will climb through mountains and then pass through the spell-binding Koosharem Valley dotted with horses and cattle where time seems to stand still. The Cowboy Country terrain of lakes, farms, cattle ranches, lush green mountains and black volcanic fields will leave you breathless as you drive through a world of wondrous bounty and desolation. Believe it or not, you are driving through the ancient caldera of a long-extinct volcano. Much of these lands are now protected by conservation easements as the ranchers work with environmentalists to preserve the natural beauty of this forgotten part of America.

You will then drop into mining country, dominated by open pit mines and monstrous machinery where sleepy Mormon towns are busily clinging to life by harvesting the earth.

Mining will soon give way to industrial strength agriculture and the character of the towns will grow softer and more pleasant. You will stop in several of these rural waysides to catch a glimpse of life in the slow lane.

And then you will be back on Interstate 15, going 80 mph with trucks and other travelers as you close the loop back to Salt Lake City where your journey began.

Along the way you will stop in the bustling farm town of Payson to walk around the outside of their heavenly new temple that rises out of the earth like a glowing white rocket ship.

After that, it's a drive through the Utah Lake Valley, the beehive state's new technology corridor, past Spanish Fork, Springville, Provo, and Orem, where large international companies are building mega factory complexes for developing and shipping goods around the world. Companies like Amazon and Google are erecting expansive service hubs in this area, taking advantage of the well-educated and homogenously-reliable Mormon workforce. You are looking at the future of America. And it's going like gangbusters in Utah.

And you will end your day in the heart of downtown Salt Lake City, roaming the streets of this curiously sterile, but endlessly interesting, heart of the Mormon. Your last stop will be at the world-famous Temple Square.

Who could ask for anything more?

How to Get There

- Drive UT 24 West. (29 miles)
- Turn right onto UT 25 North to Fish Lake. (10 miles)

After your visit to Fish Lake:

- Backtrack on UT 25 to UT 24 West and turn right. (10 miles)

- Drive UT 24 West. (40 miles**) * In the town of Sigurd, you will need to make sure you turn right to stay on UT 24.**
- When you come to I-70 just past Sigurd, take I-70 west. (7 miles)
- Take the US 50 exit to the left at the **Love's Travel Stop** which will lead you into Salina.
- In the middle of Salina, continue straight onto US 89 heading north to Gunnison. (15 miles)
- In Gunnison, you will continue straight onto UT 28 north to Nephi. (41 miles)
- Follow 1-15 N to W 600 S. (79 miles)
- Take exit 306 from I-15
- Follow w 600 S and S State Street to S Temple. (2 miles)

Where to Eat

- Breakfast - **Capitol Reef Inn & Cafe**. They have a delectable breakfast buffet with a wide assortment of fruit and other tasty items for a very reasonable price.
  https://capitolreefresort.com/dining/
- Lunch - Historic **Fish Lake Lodge** at Fish Lake
  http://www.fishlakeresorts.com/

Best Things to Do

- Eat breakfast and check out of your hotel by **8AM**.
- Stop briefly at the **Torrey Trading Post** on your left in the middle of town by the Indian teepee.
  http://www.torreytradingpost.com/
- Drive slowly through the lovely towns of **Bicknell** and **Lyman**, checking out these untouched Mormon agricultural towns that seem a bit lost out of time.
  https://en.wikipedia.org/wiki/Bicknell,_Utah
  https://en.wikipedia.org/wiki/Lyman,_Utah

- Drive to **Fish Lake** and continue past the lodges, restaurants, and marina to **Joe's Bush Boat Launch**. Get out and walk along the shores of the lovely alpine lake.
  https://www.fs.usda.gov/fishlake
- Eat lunch at the historic **Fish Lake Lodge**.
- Continue your drive north to Salt Lake City.
- Go six miles past the summit on UT 24 and stop to check out the roadside attraction on the left called the **"Indian Peace Treaty Memorial"** made of colored native stone. It is a window into the history of how the Indians and Mormons managed to peacefully coexist with one another.
- Continue through mountains and then pass through the ancient volcanic caldera of the spellbinding **Koosharem Valley.**
- Stop at **Miss Mary's Historical Museum** in Salina. This is a short, but really interesting glimpse into Utah's pioneer past. And the museum is housed in a lovely old brick building with a steeple that is worth a look even if the museum is closed.
  http://www.salinacity.org/miss-marys-museum-in-salina/
- Quick stop (you can even do it from your car) in **Gunnison** to check out the impressive **City Hall** and the historic **Casino Star Theater** on the main drag.
  http://www.gunnisoncity.org/
- Stop in the bustling town of **Payson** and walk around the **outside** of the brand spanking new **Mormon Temple**. You will see it to the right of the interstate as you are coming into the town. It looks like a white interstellar rocket. Let your eyes lead you there. But **don't try and go inside because only Mormons are allowed, and even then, you need to have had a local Mormon vouch for you and then notify the folks at the Temple that you are coming**. The outside of the Temple is well worth a brief stop. There are some lovely gardens and the grounds are open to the public.
  https://ldschurchtemples.org/payson/
- Drive to Salt Lake City.

https://www.visitsaltlake.com/

- Your final stop of the trip will be **Temple Square**. Depending on how much time you have and when you must get to the airport, will determine what you can see, but it's definitely worth the stop even if you just have a few minutes. ***https://www.templesquare.com/***
- **You cannot go inside the Temple**, but there are plenty of other fun attractions.
    - Temple Square North Visitors Center
    - Salt Lake Tabernacle
    - Church History Museum
    - Pioneer Log Cabin
    - Family History Museum
    - Brigham Young Monument
    - The Beehive House
    - Eagle Gate

Best Hikes

- There are no long hikes planned today, just short hikes around Fish Lake, the Payson Temple, and Temple Square in Salt Lake City.

Insider Tips

- The Torrey Trading Post will be your last best stop to pick up some Canyonlands souvenirs to take back home.
- There's a very good **pie** shop in Bicknell.
- There's an excellent **beef jerky** store in Gunnison.

Save Money!

- Fish Lake is **FREE!**
- Miss Mary's Museum in Salina is **FREE!**
- The Mormon Temple in Payson is **FREE!**
- Temple Square is **FREE!**

FOURTEEN DAY TRIP

PLEASE REVIEW THE "PLAN YOUR TRIP" SECTION AT THE BEGINNING OF THE BOOK.

Day One

Fly to Salt Lake City

Booking Your Flights

- Arrive in Salt Lake City by **3PM** because you have a long drive to Price, Utah after the flight.
- **WHEN YOU BOOK YOUR ROUNDTRIP TICKET TO SALT LAKE CITY YOU NEED TO MAKE SURE THAT YOUR RETURN FLIGHT DOESN'T LEAVE BEFORE 6 PM SO THAT YOU HAVE TIME THAT LAST DAY TO VISIT TEMPLE SQUARE IN SALT LAKE CITY BEFORE FLYING HOME**.

Getting Around

- See Day 1 at the beginning of the book for detailed car rental information.

How to Get There

- Drive I-80 East (170 miles) to Green River, Wyoming.
- Get on I-80 E from Crossbar Rd. (5 min (2.7 mi)
- Head northeast on Terminal Dr. (121 ft)
- Slight right toward N 3700 W. (0.2 mi)
- Turn right onto N 3700 W. (0.1 mi)
- Continue straight. (0.1 mi)
- Continue onto Crossbar Rd. (0.8 mi)
- Merge onto Terminal Dr. (0.3 mi)
- Use the left 2 lanes to take the I-80 E ramp to City Center/ Ogden/Provo. (0.7 mi)

- Keep left at the fork, follow signs for I-80 and merge onto I-80 E. (0.4 mi)
- Follow I-80 E to W Flaming Gorge Way in Green River. Take the exit toward US-30/Rock Springs from I-80 E,
- Merge onto I-80 E. (5.8 mi)
- Keep right at the fork to stay on I-80 E, follow signs for Cheyenne/Interstate 80. (5.0 mi)
- **Entering Wyoming** (159 mi*)*
- Do not take the first exit into Green River, WY
- Take Exit 89 which will lead you directly to your hotel ***http://www.cityofgreenriver.org/***

You are traveling on **America's first interstate highway**. The **Lincoln Highway** (I-80) from New York to California was opened in 1913, following two-track wagon trails whose highest point is at 8,835 feet at Sherman Hill, between Cheyenne and Laramie, where there is a giant bust of Lincoln. These days, the **speed limit is 80!**
https://www.lincolnhighwayassoc.org/

Where to Stay

- **Oak Tree Inn**, Green River, Wyoming ***http://www.guestreservations.com/oak-tree-inn-green-river/booking***
- You will find all the chain motels in Green River. It's a big regional town. So, you should be able to easily book a room online.

Camping

- **The Travel Camp** on the west side of Green River, Wyoming ***https://thetravelcamp.com/***
- **You can primitive camp anywhere you like for up to 14 days in any national forest in America for free unless it is clearly posted that you can't. It is the same for all Bureau of Land Management Lands (BLM). And most of the lands you will be passing through are either National Forest or BLM. BUT,**

not Park Service lands! You must always camp in a campground or obtain a backcountry camping permit to camp in a National Park.

- There are many dirt roads leading to primitive camping areas in the Pinyon/Juniper terrain off dirt roads along US 191 right after you turn off I-80 about six miles east of Green River. And farther down US 191 is the **Fire Hole Campground**. And all the land to the left and right of US 191 is BLM land where you can primitive camp for free.
  https://www.recreation.gov/camping/fire-hole-canyon-campground/r/campgroundDetails.do?contractCode=NRSO&parkId=70089

Where to Eat

- Dinner - **Mi Casita** in Green River in the middle of downtown on Main Street. Make sure you get there before **9PM** when they close.
  https://www.tripadvisor.com/Restaurant_Review-g60476-d3730354-Reviews-Mi_Casita-Green_River_Sweetwater_County_Wyoming.html

Best Things to Do

- Stop in **Evanston, Wyoming.**
  http://www.evanstonwy.org/
- Southern Wyoming is oil and gas country, endless expanses of rolling brown hills pin cushioned by mining equipment large and small. There are no towns, trees, or water. The sky is usually cloudy and grey. The word ***bleak*** comes to mind. And don't be surprised if it's **snowing** in late spring or early fall.
- Stop at the **Walmart Supercenter** at **Exit #5** in Evanston. Buy lawn chairs, a few cases of bottled water, groceries, snacks, and a sturdy cooler, all for a very reasonable price.
- As you exit the Walmart parking lot after buying your supplies, look to the right for a big sign, throbbing with red neon letters, on a barn-like building called **Discount Liquor**. They have

great prices and a huge selection of beer, wine, and liquor. This will be your last chance to buy **REAL** beer on the trip! In Utah, the alcohol content of beer is **capped at 3.2%** and you can only buy booze in **State Liquor Stores** which are few and far between and limited to daytime hours.

- Drive to your hotel in **Green River, WY** and eat dinner.

Insider Tips

- **Make sure that your vehicle comes equipped with GPS**. If you must pay extra, so be it, because it's worth having that very valuable assistance. For the times when you don't have an internet connection, you can use this guide book. And be sure to stop at the visitor centers in each state and pick up a **FREE!** paper state highway map.
- Here's a very valuable mapping trick to get around the times when you do not have an internet connection, using Green River and Flaming Gorge as an example. When you get up in the morning at the Oak Tree Motel, you will have a good internet connection. Open Google maps. Type in "Flaming Gorge Dam" and that area will appear on your phone. Just leave it there for future use when you are at the dam later in the day. When you get to Flaming Gorge you will not have any internet, but when you open the google map that you previously downloaded, it will still provide you with the "little blue dot" function that will follow you as you move even though you are not connected to the internet. How can that be, you ask? Because the phone is using **GPS satellite tracking** and not the internet. Yes, it's like magic. And you can use this little trick wherever you go. I use it all the time in Europe where I never have an internet connection other than cafes.
- You can also download **FREE**! map apps for your phone that will put some outstanding maps at the touch of your finger.
- Arrive in Salt Lake City by **3PM** because you have a long drive after the flight and the restaurants in Green River close at **9**. If

you are running late, then stop in Evanston, or at the huge truck stop 60 miles to the west called **Little America** for dinner. ***http://wyoming.littleamerica.com/***

- Most restaurants in Utah's small Mormon towns close by **9PM**.

Save Money!

- Stop at the **Walmart Supercenter** and **Discount Liquors** in Evanston, will save **you money** buying your essential supplies for the trip.
- Take advantage of **FREE!** Map apps for your phone or iPad.
- Download one of the many **FREE! Star Chart apps** onto your cell phone so you can use it to see what you are looking at in the night sky. This is a great way to learn the constellations.

Day Two

FLAMING GORGE DAM

Your first impression of Green River is probably going to be that it isn't very green. It looks dry as a bone and the stunted brown grass crunches under foot. It is essentially a dangerous fire trap. No one seems to notice.

This is an industrial town comprised mostly of men - white men - large, hardworking, chain-smoking drillers and miners in dirty coveralls and fluorescent yellow vests, driving the standard white pickups of the *Let's Tear It Up Clan*. The motels are filled with their muddy white F-150's.

Green River is primarily known for one thing: the industrial mining of trona and potash. Green River is the *"Trona Capital of the World"*. You can even follow the Trona Trail to the various mine sites. The largest and purest deposits of trona in the world can be found around Green River. What's trona, you ask? Trona is a sedimentary mineral, *sodium sesquicarbonate*, deposited by an ancient inland lake as it evaporated 55 million years ago. It is mined about 1,500 feet below the earth with huge 75-ton boring drills that resemble metallic dinosaurs and then processed into soda ash.

Trona is used to make almost everything in your home and to control pollution. Twelve-foot-thick beds are mined in underground cities in the nearby mountains, with maintenance shops, bathrooms, lunchrooms, electricity, and streets. Soda Ash is the primary ingredient in soap, baking soda, toothpaste, glass, glue, paper, snacks, fire extinguishers, and cattle feed. Westvaco sunk the first trona mine in 1946, right after World War II. The Church and Dwight Company opened their first sodium bicarbonate processing plant in 1986 (Arm & Hammer). Eventually there were five trona mines and four soda ash processing plants around Green River. The locals call it the "Trona Patch". So, if you have a box of baking soda in your fridge, you have a little piece of Wyoming.

To put the importance of mining in perspective, there are so many shift workers living in Green River that the City Council banned door-to-door salesman so that the night shift could sleep in peace.

Wyoming is world-renowned for its many well-preserved fossils that were deposited millions of years ago in what were once ancient sea beds. This part of America and most of the Canyonlands were transformed from oceans, to lakes, to rivers and swamps many times over. Every rock formation you will pass through during your two-week trip started as a sand dune or the bottom of some large body of water. Then they were uplifted into their current position when the continental tectonic plates smashed into one another. Wind, water, and erosion have done the rest.

Knightia, a small herring, is Wyoming's state fossil. Geologists have also found alligators, turtles, bats, plants, crayfish, beetles, dragon-flies, fig leaves, and palm fronds within the sandstone formations of southern Wyoming. And the prehistoric swamps deposited the coal which is fossilized peat. Hence the name "fossil fuel" when referring to oil, coal, and natural gas.

Early industries included the making of railroad ties and ice cut from the frozen river and placed in insulating sawdust for local use in summer.

Burnout, also known as ling, is an eel-like predatory fish not native to the Green River. Someone put the damn things in the Big Sandy Reservoir in the 1990s and now they are taking over. And just like with the snakehead fish in the Chesapeake Bay where I live, the fish-ery is becoming quite popular with the local anglers.

Non-native species, like ling, or the New Zealand Mudsnail, flourish and drive out the natives because of the dams, like the Fortenelle

and Flaming Gorge, which have created unnatural, warm water "tail water" systems that are slowly destroying the natural river system, like the vibrant Killdeer Wetlands that once thrived in the river's sweeping bends.

After your visit to Green River, you will follow the meandering Green River Valley to one of America's most impressive dams where you will do a fun hike along the Green River. It really is a luscious green!

Then, it's up into the mountains of the often-snowy Ashley National Forest with its panoramic views and big old trees.

And then you will drop out of the mountains on a winding forest road that leads you into a land of redrocks and your first glimpse of the fiery Canyonlands.

This will be a day of extremes that you will long remember!

How to Get There

- Head north. (348 ft)
- Keep right at the fork and merge onto I-80 9.4 mi)
- Take Exit 99 for US-191 S toward E Flaming Gorge Rd (0.3 mi)
- Turn right onto US-191 S. (sign for Flaming Gorge E)
- Take Exit 99 onto US 191 South. (60 miles)
- **Enter Utah**
- Follow signs to Flaming Gorge East.

After your hike in Flaming Gorge, drive to Vernal, Utah:

- Backtrack on US 191 South to Vernal, Utah. (40 miles) ***http://vernalcity.org/***

Where to Stay

- **Studio 6** in Vernal, Utah (Indoor Pool)

https://www.staystudio6.com/en/motels.ut.vernal.5032.html

- You will find all the chain motels in Vernal. It's a big regional town. So, you should be able to easily book a room online.

Camping

- **Vernal Dinosaurland KOA** in Vernal, Utah
https://koa.com/campgrounds/vernal/
- You have multiple options around Vernal to find BLM land where you can camp for **FREE!** As you are coming into Vernal from the north on US 191, you will see a right hand turn for **UT 121 (W 500 N)**; and when the farm fields end at the edge of town, go another half-mile and start looking for a dirt road in either direction because it is all BLM land where you can primitive camp for **FREE!**
- Your best option is just north of town along US 191 at a lovely oasis called **Steinaker State Park** where you will find places to primitive camp.
https://stateparks.utah.gov/parks/steinaker/

Best Places to Eat

- Breakfast - **Penny's Diner** in Green River, WY. The Oak Tree Inn motel complex sits right behind **Penny's Silver Diner**, a 24/7 flash from the sixties with Chuck Berry, The Beach Boys, and the Soul Train hit parade playing on the jukebox non-stop.
https://www.tripadvisor.com/Restaurant_Review-g60476-d3258214-Reviews-Penny_s_Diner-Green_River_Sweetwater_County_Wyoming.html
- Lunch - There is a full-service resort just before the Flaming Gorge Dam on the left called **Dutch John Resort** with gas, hotel, campground, camping gear, general store, and a pretty good steakhouse.
https://dutchjohnresort.com/

- Dinner - **Plaza Mexicana** in Vernal, Utah. This is where the locals dine, and it offers good Tex-Mex food at a very reasonable price.
  https://www.yelp.com/biz/plaza-mexicana-vernal

Best Things to Do

- Finish breakfast and get on the road by **9AM**.
- Your first stop in Green River after a yummy breakfast at the diner is the **Green River Visitor Center** (right across from the diner) on the west end of town where there are many informative outside exhibits about mining, wild horses, and the ecology of the Green River Basin. Inside, there are some very interesting Western artifacts and natural history books and – always a big plus – clean bathrooms. Spend a few minutes on one of the many benches overlooking the stark, yet lovely, **Green River** and the recently restored **Kildeer Wetlands**.
  http://www.grchamber.com/
- Your next stop is the **Sweetwater County Museum** which is housed in the **old Post Office on Main Street** across from the town's most popular Mexican restaurant **Mi Casita**. This amazing museum is **FREE!** and is well worth an hour perusing its contents before taking an amusing walk around town. They have an outstanding museum, gift shop, bookstore, and library where they still do **FREE! genealogy research**. The museum has some thought-provoking exhibits about petrified forests and dinosaurs; prehistoric and Native American people; trappers (beaver and bison) like Jedediah Smith, Kit Carson, and Jim Bridger; explorers and pathfinders like John Fremont, geologic surveyor Dr. Ferdinand Hayden, and John Wesley Powell; pioneers and settlers heading west to Oregon; Mormons and gold seekers (many trails went through Sweetwater); the Pony Express and stagecoaches; railroads like the Union Pacific; commercial steamboat operations along the Green River like the behemoth *Comet;* cattle ranchers, farmers, homesteaders and crazy coal miners; the Chinese "Massacre" on September 2, 1885 and the burning of Green River's Chinatown; the propensity of global

cuisine due to miners coming from all over the globe; and the building of the Lincoln Highway from New York to California in 1913, following two-track wagon trails whose highest point is at 8,835 feet at Sherman Hill, between Cheyenne and Laramie, where there is a giant bust of Lincoln ... **The Human Migration**.

- After your stop at the Museum, cross main street and walk to your right for a couple of blocks which will lead you down by the railroad tracks along **West Railroad Avenue**. This is where you will find Wyoming's most unique building, **The Brewery**, an old German brewery, now a local bar, erected in 1900, with stone beer kegs and chalices crowning its roof like castle ramparts. You can see The Brewery from Main Street.
https://en.wikipedia.org/wiki/Sweetwater_Brewery
- Continue walking left on West Railroad Avenue past the town's many dive bars. Mile-long "double tracked" trains are constantly cruising through the town. Green River is the **main switching yard for the Union Pacific trains** rumbling through that part of the country day and night. The buildings literally shake with each passing train. Green River is also home to one of only two remaining **pedestrian bridges over railroad tracks** in America. Railroad buffs come from all over the world to see it and snap their pictures of a bygone era.
http://www.cityofgreenriver.org/index.aspx?NID=244
- On the far side of the bridge are stone steps leading down to the river and two blocks away (straight ahead) is **Expedition Island**, located in a city park connected to a paved **Greenbelt trail along the Green River**, where the Powell expeditions departed in 1869 and 1871, to explore the unmapped Green and Colorado rivers. John Wesley Powell, the one-armed Civil War veteran, explorer, and founder of the USGS is one of my all-time favorite heroes.
https://www.tourwyoming.com/explore/sightseeing-and-attractions/expedition-island.html
- After checking out Expedition Island, retrace your steps past **Evers Park** and back into town across the railroad bridge.

Continue straight on **North 1st East Street** for one block to **East Flaming Gorge Way**. At the intersection, look to your right at the **Historic Hotel Tomahawk** which was undergoing a full restoration in 2017. Take a left on East Flaming Gorge way and return to your car.

- Stop in at the Flaming Gorge Visitor Center and learn about the history, wildlife, and cultural resources of this unique natural gem. And be sure to check the weather and local conditions. ***https://utah.com/flaming-gorge***
- Hike the **Little Hole National Scenic Trail** along the **Green River**. It really is green!
- After your hike, drive back **across the top of the dam** and begin your long climb out of the gorge on the twisting highway that will lead you up into the often-stormy Uinta Mountains, stopping briefly to snap some photos at a space age ***Jetsons Bridge*** with "NO CLIFF DIVING " signs posted on the edge of the canyon.

Best Hikes

- Hike around the town of Green River, Wyoming.
- **Little Hole National Scenic Trail** - This 8-mile long trail begins at the bottom of the 510′ Flaming Gorge Dam and runs along the left edge of the Green River. The trail is well-maintained and very easy to follow. It's an out and back hike and you can determine how far you want to go. If you walk down river for two miles, then it's a four-mile hike. The trail is in a deep canyon with towering rock walls framing the river that is filled with fishermen in their colorful dories and abundant wildlife, like soaring hawks and golden eagles. Look for river trips going downstream for day trips. And this stretch of the river is known for its colorful dories piloted by commercial river guides who take fishermen through one of the best trout fishing rivers in America. ***http://www.flaminggorgecountry.com/Little-Hole-National-Scenic-Trail***

Insider Tips

- About two miles past the Dutch John Resort, and right before the road drops down into the canyon that leads to the dam, you will see a sign on the right for a **Scenic Overlook**. Drive for about a mile to an amazing view of the lake, the dam, and the surrounding landscape.
- Getting to the best trailhead for your hike along the Green River is a bit tricky. Follow the **River Access sign** to the left just before the dam. You can't park at the trailhead, so you should drive past the first large parking area right after a sharp right turn on the road down to the river and then pass through the usually unattended entrance station. Park in the **FREE!** lot on the left by a **trash can covered in stickers** where there is a short, steep and rocky trail that leads down to the **Little Hole National Scenic Trail** along the Green River.
- If you want to avoid the steep trail down to the river that is littered with loose rocks, just park and then walk down the road to the dam where you can snap some incredible photos. Then look to your left, just past the boat launch, and you will see the river trail.
- Bring a towel to go swimming. Yes, the river is quite cold because it has just been released from the bottom of the tall dam. But on a hot day, it is very refreshing. Look for places along the trail where you can get down to the water. But be careful that you stay along the bank in the eddy line (the current moving back up-river) and don't get into the fast-moving current which will sweep you down-river.
- The Uinta Mountains are a lightning rod for nasty weather. **It can snow at any time of the year,** like it was doing at the end of August 2017, when I last visited the area. The road is steep and windy, and there are big log trucks. If the weather is bad, **take your time and be safe**. And as soon as your drop down out of the mountains, you will be in a redrock oven for the rest of the trip. So, enjoy your brief stop in the mountains. There are

many pull offs where you can get out and snap some wonderful photos of the forest.
https://www.fs.usda.gov/ashley

- Full moons, sunrise, sunset, and stargazing are **FREE!** And there is no better place on earth to see the stars than Canyonlands. The International Dark-Sky Association works to protect the night skies for present and future generations, and they produce a map each year showing light pollution zones around the globe. They also designate "Dark-Sky Parks", of which Canyonlands is one. So, stargazing in southeastern Utah is pretty stellar (bad pun intended), and you should take advantage of it almost every night by driving out into the high desert and watching the stars for a few hours while drinking a few frosty beverages.
http://www.darksky.org/

Save Money!

- The Oak Tree Inn Motel offers a **FREE!** complimentary breakfast at Penny's Silver Diner, but you can only order the standard American breakfast. **Read the small print on the voucher** because if you don't order precisely, you will end up paying for the meal.
- The Green River Visitor Center is **FREE!** And so is the parking.
- The Sweetwater County Museum is **FREE!** And so is the parking.
- Before you leave the Green River and Sweetwater County Visitor Centers, pick up the **FREE! park maps**, especially for the areas where you will be traveling next.
- Most of the chain motels offer a **FREE!** breakfast, usually consisting of: cereal, yogurt, toast, pastries, fruit, milk, juice, coffee, and tea.

Day Three

DINOSAUR NATIONAL MONUMENT

Vernal started out as a farming and ranching town. These days it's the regional economic hub of northeast Utah and the gateway to Dinosaur National Monument. It has morphed into a pretty bustling place with big box store EVERYTHING! And there are life size amusement park dinosaurs scattered up and down Main Street. It's cheesy and goofy in a sort happy-go-lucky way and it's impossible not to stop and snap a few photos. Vernal has clearly staked its future on the wonderful world of dinosaurs.

After breakfast and before heading over to Dinosaur National Monument, you should spend a few hours exploring Vernal because there are some hidden gems in a lot of these Mormon towns. You just have to get out of your car and do some exploring. Otherwise, you will probably miss them.

The big tourist attraction in Vernal is a hokey-looking place in the middle of town called Dinosaur Land. Given that you will soon be hiking around Dinosaur National Monument, where they showcase the fossilized remains of REAL dinosaurs, the idea of paying to see plastic replicas is a bit absurd. For that same reason, it is probably a waste of your limited time to pay to go into the world-renowned Field Museum of Natural History with it's big, snarling Tyrannosaurus Rex out in front. Go see the real thing!

Your visit to Dinosaur National Monument will be a trip back into ancient time. You will do some amazing hikes and follow the Green River through a lush valley filled with geological wonders and the incredible march of human history.

Then it's back in the car and a scenic drive through the Green River Valley and its farms and sleepy little farming towns before heading back into the mountains through meadows lined with seesaw oil derricks. And you will finish your amazing drive by dropping into the strange industrial city of Price, Utah where mining rules.

By the end of your day, your head will be spinning as you try and fathom the many incredible things you have learned and seen on your second day in Canyonlands.

And you're just getting started!

How to Get There

- Drive US 40 East (Main Street) out of Vernal. (13 miles)
- Turn left on UT 149 to the Dinosaur National Monument Visitor Center. (4 miles)

After your visit to the Park drive to Price, Utah:

- Backtrack to Vernal and turn left on US 191. (44 miles)
- Turn left onto US-191 S/US-6 E. (9.5 miles)

  Take exit 240 toward U.S. 6 Business Loop/Price.
  http://www.priceutah.net/

Where to Stay

- **Super 8** in Price, Utah (Indoor Pool) ***https://www.wyndhamhotels.com/super-8/price-utah/super-8-price/overview?CID=LC:SE::GGL:RIO:National:07207&iata=00065402***
- You will find all the chain motels in Price. It's a fairly big regional town. So, you should be able to easily book a room online.

Camping

- **El Rancho Motel** & RV Campground in Price ***https://mapcarta.com/23423310***

- Your best option for **FREE!** Primitive camping is going to be a bit tricky because Price is a pretty big town and it will take some work to get to the nearest BLM land. Take the **South Carbon Avenue** exit (UT 10) off US 191. Go a short distance and take a right on **Byproducts Road**. Take your first right onto **South Fairgrounds Road** which will parallel US 191 in the direction (north) you previously came. Go a mile or so and when the road starts to make a big sweeping turn to the left, go straight onto **W 250 S**. Go another mile and start looking for a gravel road on the right or the left. To be honest, I would just camp in a the El Rancho and avoid dealing with the hassle of finding a BLM camping spot in such an active area.

Where to Eat

- Breakfast - **7/11 Ranch Restaurant** in Vernal, Utah ***http://www.7-11ranchrestaurant.com/***
- Lunch - Snacks
- Dinner - **Frontier Grill** in Roosevelt, Utah. This is not great dining. But don't let the bad review dissuade you. They have homemade bread and honey butter, and they offer some nice salads. I especially liked the fruit salad. By the time you get to Roosevelt you are going to be hungry. And it is the largest town you will pass through. There are some other very average restaurants in town if you don't like the Frontier. But I think the inside décor which is sort of like the inside of someone's home is worth the stop. It's vintage small-town Mormon and quite amusing. ***https://www.tripadvisor.com/Restaurant_Review-g57116-d661844-Reviews-Frontier_Grill-Roosevelt_Utah.html***

Best Things to Do

- Eat breakfast by **9AM**.
- After breakfast at the 7/11 Ranch Restaurant, walk around the town center where you will find an amazing abundance of hanging **flower baskets and planters filled with purple petunias** along the entire length of Main Street (and every other Mormon town you will travel through). They also have little **brass**

interpretive signs that tell some very interesting stories about the buildings of note. For instance, the bank building was built with bricks delivered in small boxes by the U.S. Postal Service. And it precipitated the national policy of charging for mail by **weight**. Up until that point there was just a standard fee for any package.

- In the middle of town along Main Street you will see a huge **Veterans Memorial** - every Mormon town has some sort of Veterans Memorial. This one is the biggest you will encounter on the trip. The centerpiece features the standard soldier sculpture, surrounded by brass plaques, white marble tablets engraved with the names of the townsfolk killed in battle, all ringed by American flags. But it also has a green Huey helicopter gunship on stilts that was flown in Vietnam by a local pilot. It's very cool.
- Sitting behind the Veterans Memorial is the **Uintah Heritage Museum** right next to a pretty public park. It looks like the kind of place where you would have to pay but it is **FREE!** You can easily spend over an hour checking it out. Amazingly, you will find no dinosaurs. The museum highlights what life in Vernal was like over the years. They have recreated a mercantile store; the town's old switchboard and teletype machine; purple glassware; military heroes; looted Indian artifacts; all things cowboy and horsey; the sturdy red safe from the Vernal Drug Company and soda fountain; the organ from the first Mormon church; photographic equipment used by the town's famous camera bug **Lou Thorne** who chronicled the lives of the locals and Indians; early commercial river runners like **Bus Hatch**; a truly weird **First Ladies of the White House doll exhibit**, ending with Nancy Reagan (the lady who made the dolls died before the Clintons); odd landscape paintings; old wooden wheelchairs, typewriters, household appliances, furniture, pocket watches, musical instruments, and wood stoves; a barbershop; the steel door from the town jail; and, of course, lots and lots of guns. Each month they feature a special exhibit, like elaborate quilts made by the local ladies.

https://www.uintahmuseum.org/

I really can't say enough about these little museums in many of the larger Mormon towns. *Museums* is perhaps too highbrow a word to describe them. I'm sure that any curator at a fancy-pants museum would find them, at best, *amusing*, because they are for the most part just a curious assemblage of items that define life in their little corner of the Beehive State. Many of the exhibits have been donated by local families. And a lot of the items are dusty and a bit threadbare. But they are *genuine*. And in their own convoluted way, they tell some very important and truly touching stories.

Dinosaur National Monument

It's only about seventeen miles from Vernal to Dinosaur National Monument. US 40 will take you through an Edenesque valley. Irrigation from the Green River has turned the high desert of northeastern Utah into lush fields of alfalfa, melons, and cow crops, their tall pivot pumps blasting rainbow spray into the air like money dropping from the sky. This vision of manmade paradise extends south and west from Vernal for over 100 miles. I don't know this for a fact, but from the looks of it, the Mormon farmers and ranchers are busily sucking the Green River aquifer dry like there is no tomorrow. Maybe they know something we don't.

The first Dinosaur National Monument was established in **1915** to protect the quarry and about **eighty acres** around it, but visitors and locals alike lobbied for the park to be expanded to include the nearby river canyons that had been carved by the **Green and Yampa Rivers**, and in 1938, **President Franklin D. Roosevelt** increased the monument's size to over **210,000 acres**.

"Dinosaur National Monument contains famous fossil finds, dramatic river canyons, intriguing petroglyphs, and endless opportunities for adventure. Whether you delight in the challenge of a strenuous hike to spectacular views, the thrill of rafting through a twisting canyon, or sitting quietly and watching the sunset, Dinosaur National Monument offers a myriad of activities for you to enjoy. The hardest part may be choosing which auto tour, trail, overlook, or historic area to explore!

Start your journey at one of the monument's visitor centers. Drive the Tour of the Tilted Rocks. Experience one of the monument's many hiking trails. Soak up the monument's wilderness on a river rafting trip. Discover dinosaur and other fossils. Join a ranger for a guided program. Park staff offer talks, walks, junior ranger, evening and night sky programs. Stay overnight at a campground. Enjoy night skies while stargazing. Or just lounge by the river and take in all that Dinosaur National Monument has to offer."
-NPS Brochure
https://www.nps.gov/dino/index.htm

- After the very informative thirty minute movie at the Visitor Center, hop on the **FREE!** shuttle for a five minute ride up the steep hill to the **dinosaur bone quarry** inside a brand new air conditioned glass building encasing the hillside where in 1909, **Dr. Douglass from Carnegie Melon, in Pittsburgh**, excavated over **1,500 dinosaurs** that died **150 million years ago** during the Jurassic Period after getting stuck in what was once a muddy river bend, but which now is a colossal sandstone mountain jutting up into the sky.
- Upon returning to the Visitor Center purchase the ***Auto Guidebook for the Cub Creek Road*** for **$1** and take the **24-mile (round trip) Tilted Rock Scenic Drive**. There are **15 stops** and the best ones are: The **Swelter Shelter Petroglyphs**, **Desert Voices Trail**, **Chew Ranch**; **Turtle Rock**, and **Elephant Toes Butte**.
- You should incorporate either the **Sound of Silence Trail** or the **Desert Voices Trail** into your drive because they are both accessed from the tour route along Cub Creek Road.

Tilted Rocks Driving Tour Highlights

- At the 0.9-mile mark there is one of the monument's oldest prehistoric ruins, **"Swelter Shelter"** (named by the folks who excavated the site in the middle of summer). It is 7,000 years old and dates to the **Desert Archaic Period**. There are also pictographs and petroglyphs on the shelter's walls made about 1,000 years ago by the **Fremont Culture**.

https://en.wikipedia.org/wiki/Fremont_culture

- At the 1.8-mile mark is the trailhead for the **Sound of Silence Trail**. The **Desert Voices Trail** connects to the Sound of Silence Trail, so if you have time and are feeling ambitious you can do them both for a long loop trail.
- At the 5.8-mile mark is a spectacular overlook with a panoramic view of the **Cub Creek Valley** and the multi-colored **Split Mountain**.
- At the 7.2-mile mark is a short gravel road to the right that leads to **Placer Point**, where miners sluiced for gold against the river-bank in the 1930s.
- At the 7.6-mile mark is the **Chew Ranch**, a private inholding within the Monument, where the Chew family raise alfalfa, corn, sheep, horses and cattle.
- At the 9.4-mile mark is **"Turtle Rock"** in the Entrada Sandstone.
- At the 10-mile mark go left to **"Elephant Toes Butte"** in the Nugget Sandstone.
- At the **10.7-mile mark the asphalt ends** and things really begin to get interesting, starting with an incredible **rock art panel** perched along the left side of **Cub Creek Road**. There is a short trail starting to the left of the parking area. Check it out! The panels have some amazing glyphs, including a **big shiny lizard** and **Kokopelli, the flute player,** jamming to the lizard's left.
- The last stop will be at Josie's Cabin in the shadow of **Split Mountain. Josephine Bassett Morris** was larger than life - like something out of a movie like "True Grit". Josie settled at **Hog Canyon Spring in 1914**, after five crash-and-burn marriages. She raised and butchered cattle, pigs, chickens and geese. Her large garden provided her with vegetables and fruits. She had no electricity and heated her home with a wood burning stove. Her light came from an oil lamp. She was totally self-sufficient. She was also friends with the outlaw **Butch Cassidy** and was accused (but never convicted) of rustling cattle. Josie

was a wily woman indeed and not to be trifled with. When she bumped heads with the **Utah water laws** that denied her the right to use the Hog Spring water on her own land because it drained into the larger **Cub Creek**, which another rancher had rights to, Josie found a loophole in the water rights law that would allow her to use Hog Spring as long as she made sure that it never reached Cub Creek. Josie's property is dotted with dirt impoundments where she diverted the water away from Cub Creek. In the winter of 1964, while feeding her horse, she slipped on some ice and broke her hip. She dragged herself into her home and waited for help. She had no telephone or any way to signal that she was dying. It was days before some friends from Vernal stopped by. As they were taking her to the hospital she said she had a feeling she would never see her beloved ranch ever again. And she was right. Josie died that spring at the age of 89.

Best Hikes

- **Sound of Silence Trail** - The trail begins two miles east of the Quarry Visitor Center along the **Tilted Rocks Auto Tour on Cub Creek Road**. This is a 3-mile loop trail through high desert and slickrock with outstanding cross-section views of the park's twisted geology, along with sweeping views of Split Mountain. This is the trail that I would recommend that you do given the limited time that you have. (3.2 miles - 2 hours)
- **Desert Voices Trail** - The trail begins four miles east of the Quarry Visitor Center at the Split Mountain Boat Ramp. The trail runs through high desert and slickrock with outstanding cross-section views of the park's twisted geology, with sweeping views of Split Mountain. It connects to the Sound of Silence Trail if you want to do a longer hike. (1.5 miles - 1 hour)
  https://www.nps.gov/dino/planyourvisit/hikingtrails.htm

Insider Tips

- You should always stop **first** at the Visitor Center when you arrive at a National Park or National Monument. You will get the latest weather information, trail maps and conditions, road work, find out about the ranger talks and tours, and learn about the park through very informative natural history exhibits and films. It's all **FREE!** as part of your entrance fee, so take advantage of these valuable tools. And many of the parks produce a **seasonal newspaper** that is filled with all sorts of cool information about what's happening in the park. There is a unique dinosaur quarry at the Visitor Center where you can see how they excavated the dinosaurs. Allow at least an hour for this highly informative attraction.

- In the little town of **Duchesne**, it is **easy to miss the left hand turn for US 191 South** which is in the middle of the sleepy town.
  https://en.wikipedia.org/wiki/Duchesne,_Utah
- After Duchesne, you will leave the green farm fields of the **Green River Basin** and head up into the **Manti-La Sal Mountains** where mining rules the land. There are oil derricks dotting the landscape like a rocky pincushion. The drive through the **Manti-La Sal National Forest** is a white-knuckler that seems to go on forever before you finally drop into the creepy town of **Price, Utah**, where all the ore that's mined in the region is processed twenty-four hours a day. At night, it looks like Mordor in "The Hobbit". The last ten miles or so of this drive are winding and steep and you will need to drive slowly, especially in bad weather.
  https://www.fs.usda.gov/mantilasal

Save Money!

- There is plenty of on-street parking in the center of Vernal along Main Street where all day parking is **FREE!**
- **FREE!** Heritage Museum in Vernal.
- Before you leave the Vernal Visitor Center, pick up the **FREE! park maps**, especially for the areas where you will be traveling next.

- **Annual Pass** - Purchase an Annual Pass **at the entrance station** when you enter Dinosaur National Monument, which will save you $20 in the long run because you won't have to pay $25 every time you enter another national park or monument during the trip (there will be 5). The pass costs $80 and is good in any National Park, National Monument, or National Recreation Area in the country **for a whole year**.
  https://www.nps.gov/planyourvisit/passes.htm
- **Senior Pass** - If you are a US citizen or resident and 62 years or older you can get the best deal in recreation. A Senior Pass costs only **$80 for a lifetime pass**. It enables free admission for your entire carload to National Parks, National Monuments, and many other fee areas managed by other federal agencies. **You can purchase your Senior Pass at the entrance station and the price is the same as online.**
  https://www.nps.gov/planyourvisit/senior-pass-changes.htm

Day Four

THE WEDGE & SAN RAFAEL RIVER

The larger Mormon towns, like Price, have all grown by leaps and bounds. When I say *grown*, I mean they now have sprawling Walmarts and Home Depots, which, of course, have wreaked havoc on the mom and pop businesses in the smaller towns.

And for most of the little Mormon towns of northeast Utah the past is prologue. It's guns, hunting, high school football, and the church. Folks seem happy and satisfied. Progress is measured by the passing of seasons. And it's "Groundhog Day" forevermore.

The oddest thing about Price is that it has several highway interchange overpasses. Yes, I know, they are all over a lot of urban America, but not in rural Utah. In fact, the closest interchanges are far to the north up in Provo. And what makes it doubly odd is the fact that there really isn't that much traffic. In fact, other than the ore mills, the whole town appears to be pretty much abandoned.

Price looks surreal at night with all of its off-world mines, and in the light of day downtown Price isn't much better: grid-numbered, wide as a runway streets lined with concrete drainage sluices for when it flash floods; parched cottonwoods wilting in the broilarama sun; shanty shacks and houses of brown brick dripping with incredible poverty; untended yards of brown vegetation doing their best to smother the toy-littered porches and yards; desperate trailer parks; a noisy train rumbling through the heart of the sleepy city center at all hours; dusty pickups; many structures adorned with large American flags; the war memorial statue honoring the fallen dead who served their country with honor; and shuttered stores that look as if they were abandoned in a hurry, like the Anasazi fleeing some unforeseen disaster. The people move slow, are exceedingly friendly

and courteous, love to jabber away, and will always ask you where you are from. It's just a thoroughly depressing picture, like life in a sunbaked quicksand limbo. But it has the services you need and it's worth seeing the REAL Utah.

This is going to be a very special day. After checking out the sights in Price, you are going to get WAY off the beaten track and see places that no tourists ever get to. You will be driving on all-weather gravel roads appropriate for any vehicle other than those with low clearance or during and after a bad storm. And it is unlikely that the road signs will have the names of the roads you are driving. You will always be wondering where the hell you are. Google maps won't work. You will probably be a little outside your comfort zone. And when you finally return to civilization the gravel road will magically end at Interstate 70. This is not for the faint of heart. But I have done this route in a Toyota passenger car. Pay very close attention to the distances between your turns and the brown BLM signs. They are spot on. If you take your time, and make sure you are closely following the road log directions, it will be well worth the effort. And it will definitely be one of the days you remember the most vividly from your Southwest trip.

If this sounds like a bit too much, then just push on from Price and go directly to Moab. And then add another day when you are at Capitol Reef. There are days and days of hikes to do there.

But for those who want to have a real adventure, buckle up and let's go exploring!

How to Get There

- Drive UT 10 South and UT 155 South to Center Street in the little town of Cleveland, Utah. (21 miles)
- Turn left on **Center Street** which is also **County Road 204**. (As you are leaving town you will pass a large sandstone and black metal sign on right featuring a saluting Indian)

- At the triangle, turn left onto **South Flat Bus Route**. (0.3-mile mark)
- Turn right onto **County Road 208**. (1.35-mile mark)
- **During your drive you will encounter brown BLM signs directing you to The Wedge. You will encounter your first sign at the 3.4-mile mark. When in doubt, always stay on the main (most traveled) road.**
- Turn right at the 'T' intersection (5.5-mile mark)
- You will come to a major intersection at the **Buckhorn Well Rest Area** with bathrooms, picnic area, and interpretive signs where you will go slightly to the right, following the sign to **The Wedge**. You will pass the entrance to the rest area which will be on your left. (13-mile mark)
- You will pass another sign to **The Wedge**. (19.5-mile mark)
- The road narrows but is still well-suited for passenger vehicles. (21.5-mile mark)
- The **Wedge Overlook** (23.5-mile mark)

After checking out one of the Southwest's most amazing views, follow the gravel road to the left along the rim for 0.5 miles to some picnic tables on the point overlooking the Little Grand Canyon and the San Juan River. Eat your lunch at the picnic tables in the dispersed campground (no water & no services!)

- Backtrack to the Buckhorn Well Rest Area (10.5 miles)
- At the rest area intersection, turn right onto **Buckhorn Draw Road**. There is a brown wooden road sign for **Buckhorn Draw and I-70**.

* Begin a new road log, starting at the road junction. *

- The road will soon start to drop into a spectacular canyon and you will come to the amazing **Buckhorn Panel** of rock art on the left. There is a big BLM sign. (8-mile mark)

- Stay on **Buckhorn Draw Road (County Road 332)** to the **San Rafael Bridge** which is one of the first cable supported bridges to span the San Rafael River. (12-mile mark)

After your brief hike along the river:

- Cross the San Rafael River and continue for 19 miles on **County Road 332** which is always the main road heading straight to the south. About two miles before the end, the road will begin to turn to the right and soon become a paved road paralleling I-70. This is **Temple Mountain Road** and will lead you to the **Exit 131** interchange where you will go under I-70 and then turn left on I-70 east to Green River.
- Head east on I-70 to Green River, Utah. (30 miles) ***http://greenriverutah.com/***

Where to Stay

- **Motel 6** in Green River, Utah ***https://www.motel6.com/en/motels.ut.green-river.4678.html***
- You will find all the chain motels in Green River. It's a big regional town. So, you should be able to easily book a room online.

Camping

- **Green River KOA** ***https://koa.com/campgrounds/green-river/***
- Finding **FREE!** Primitive camping on BLM land around Green River is easy. Drive east on Main Street to the interstate. Go under the overpass until the pavement turns to gravel and turn left. Drive for a little over a mile to a bluff overlooking the highway with panoramic views in every direction. You are now on federal BLM land, which means that you can pretty much go where you like and camp for **FREE!**

Where to Eat

- Breakfast - **Big Moe's** in Price, Utah ***https://www.yelp.com/biz/big-moes-eatery-and-bakery-price***
- Lunch - Snacks. You will be in the back of beyond from morning until late afternoon and there is no place at The Wedge to get lunch. You might want to stop at Subway or one of the sandwich places in Price, Utah before you leave town and pack a lunch in your cooler, so you can picnic at The Wedge.
- Dinner - Ray's Tavern in Green River, Utah. Local favorite! ***https://www.facebook.com/RaysTavern/***

Best Things to Do

- Check out of your motel and get on the road by **8AM**. ***http://www.priceutah.net/***
- After breakfast it's a two-minute drive over to the **Utah State University Eastern Prehistoric Museum**. The museum, a large ornate building with snarling dinosaurs and Indian sculptures outside, is hard to miss. On-street parking is **FREE!** but they charge $10 per person to get into the museum. It is well worth it! They have two floors with **archaeology** on the right side of the museum and two floors covering **paleontology** on the left.
- The **archaeology section** features: fascinating exhibits and dioramas showing prehistoric life through a multitude of artifacts; Paleoindian migration panels; a pack rat midden from **Dutch John** that illustrate how the climate has changed over millennia; a mockup of the Archaic dwelling at Polar Mesa dating back to BC 2040; an amazing replica of a **Fremont** pit house; medicinal and edible plants; a hide teepee; a **Kennewick Man** skull from a middle-aged guy who died 9,500 years ago; a very rare mud granary found on the **Wilcox Ranch** in Range Creek, Utah; a model of **Hovenweep Castle**; the **"Vision of Washakie"** elk skin painting by the Shoshone Chief Charlie Washakie; relics from prehistoric daily life, like baskets and sandals; weapons like bows and arrows; a very interesting

display showing the time sequence for projectile points, starting with a **Clovis Point** dating from **BC 12,000**; and realistic paintings made to look exactly like the **Great Gallery** rock art panel in **Horseshoe Canyon.**

- The **paleontology section** is equally intriguing with real and imagined turtles; the steel trap **Dunkleoteus** that possessed the most powerful bite of any fish ever known; the armadillo-like, super-sized **Glyptodons** with their body armor and stone tails with sharp spikes; big-foot, duck-billed **Hadrosaurs** that lived along the western coast of the **Cretaceous Seaway** (where Utah sits today) and whose massive footprints were found deep in the coal mines of Carbon County, giant clams, snails, and oysters; a huge assortment of dinosaur eggs; a host of different spike-horned and armored **Ceratops**; the monstrous **Deinosuchus**, known as the "Crocodile King of Utah", which was not related to crocodiles or alligators; armored grass eaters like **Ankylosaurs**; a giant blue **sea scorpion** that roamed the ancient seas 450 million years ago; a thirty-feet-long behemoth **Alisaurus** meat eater that terrorized what is now **Grand Staircase Escalante National Monument** 72 million years ago; and, of course, the razor-clawed **Utahraptor**, a velociraptor like the pack of gangbangers that brought mayhem and carnage in the movie "Jurassic Park". They also have some great exhibits about the **1927** excavation of the nearby **Cleveland-Lloyd Quarry**; the science of **paleontology**; how the earth and Eastern Utah was formed; and twisted geology. The coolest thing about the museum is that whether it is an old Indian pot or a dinosaur they are showcasing, and regardless of the provenance, most were **discovered in Utah**. ***http://usueastern.edu/museum/***
- Drive south on UT 10 to the little farming village of **Cleveland, Utah** and head east (left) on Center Street which quickly turns to gravel when you leave town. The drive to **The Wedge** is easier than the forbidding directions above might sound. At every big intersection there is either a wooden BLM sign with the mileage to The Wedge, or, when in doubt, you should just stay on the

main dirt road. It takes about forty-five minutes to get to your destination at the **Wedge Overlook**. The views from the Wedge Overlook are absolutely breathtaking as you stand on the edge of what is referred to as the "Little Grand Canyon" looking down into a world of multi-colored, tortured and fractured redrock. It looks like a layer cake that has been sliced by God with a really big knife. Way down in the canyon bottom runs the twisting ribbon of water known as the **San Rafael River**. You might want to go for a walk along the rim to the end of the plateau that resembles the flight deck of an aircraft carrier in the clouds. There are no signs of human **ANYTHING** as far as the eye can see. And the silence is all encompassing. You will feel like the only person on the earth.
http://sanrafaelswellguide.com/the-wedge-overlook/

- Drive back to the **Buckhorn Well Rest Area** at a major intersection of dirt roads where there are bathrooms, a picnic area and about forty flashy color panels inviting you to visit many local attractions around spectacular Utah - even places like Zion National Park that are quite far away. Check out the old Buckhorn Well water pump exhibit, and just across the road to the north you can pose in front of a metal art installation standing off in the sagebrush flat, depicting a string of pack horses heading to god only knows where. It's hard to understand why the state or the county built such an expansive (and expensive) rest stop and picnic area in what is by any standard the absolute middle of nowhere. I guess hope springs eternal.
- Turn right at the rest area and follow the **Buckhorn Draw Road** (**County Road 322**). It will quickly begin dropping into a magnificent gorge. You are essentially driving through the canyon you had been gazing into from the rim of the Wedge. The road follows the bone-dry **Buckhorn Wash**, twisting like a bobsled run, the red and brown sandstone walls closing in on you the deeper you travel. And I can say without hesitation that Buckhorn Draw rivals any national park I have ever seen other than the Grand Canyon. It is stunningly majestic.
http://www.emerycounty.com/travel/buckhornwash.html

- Your next stop is about eight miles from the Buckhorn Well Rest Area. It's the football field long **Buckhorn Wash Petroglyph Panel** where the weirdly cool rock art figures have been pecked and painted over the course of millennia by a host of Anasazi artists. There are two distinct cultures and art forms at work across the shiny brown face of the smooth **Wingate Sandstone** walls. People of the **Fremont Culture** used small stones to **chisel** their symbolic drawings of bighorn sheep and spiders about a thousand years ago. But most of the panel is comprised of pictographs that were **painted** by artists of the **Barrier Canyon Culture** onto their rock canvas more than 2000 years ago. These drawings are like something from an acid flashback, featuring space men and spirits, some with large holes through their hearts and crotches. What the hell were these boys and girls trying to say? Their meaning remains a mystery. ***http://climb-utah.com/SRS/buckhorn.htm***
- Continue down the Buckhorn Draw Road which winds ever deeper, passing through **Furniture Draw** and **Calf Canyon**. Take the time to stop and take in the monumental landscape. Humans are but tiny specks in this giant world of redrock buttes.
- It's four miles from the Buckhorn Rock Art Panel to the **San Rafael River** and the **San Rafael River Bridge** which was erected by the **Civilian Conservation Corps** between **1935 and 1937** under the direction of the Division of Grazing. **It is the last remaining suspension bridge in Utah**. At the dedication ceremony, the **Utah Governor Henry H. Blood**, was joined by **2,000 people**, and the local paper heralded: "Mystery lands now opened." The wooden and steel-cable bridge was constructed to give the local ranchers a safe way to get their cattle and sheep across the often-treacherous **San Rafael River**. The **167-feet-long** bridge opened up thousands of acres of land for winter grazing. Keep your eyes open for **Desert Bighorn Sheep**. Grazing permits have been discontinued to maintain a healthy desert bighorn sheep population that were there long before the cows. It is locally referred to as the **Swinging Bridge**. A newer bridge has been constructed for vehicular traffic, but

the old Swinging Bridge can still be walked across. Camping facilities are provided at the **San Rafael Bridge Recreation Site** adjacent to the San Rafael River. The recreation site is bordered by a lofty sandstone escarpment to the north and large buttes to the east and west. Camping facilities at San Rafael Bridge include tent pads, picnic tables, toilets, and fire rings. No drinking water is available. No reservations are taken for this campground and you just put your money for camping in a metal fee box.

- Park by the bridge and walk around. There is a sandy, brushy trail along the far side of the river.
  http://www.gjhikes.com/2014/01/san-rafael-bridge.html
- Continue driving south on Buckhorn Wash Road to **I-70** and then head **east on I-70** to **Green River, Utah.**
- Once you have settled in at your hotel, head on over to **Ray's Tavern** just off Main Street in the middle of town. They specialize in fresh salads, **big** burgers, grilled meat, and cold Coronas. You will rarely see tourists in the place. It's mostly river runners, cowboys, and bikers. The walls are decorated with pictures of wave-crashing, boat smothering, Grand Canyon river trips. Make sure you check out the bathroom in the back that is just past the two pool tables. Look to your right in the corner and you will see a curious sight along the back wall. There is an old phone booth, and inside there is a Superman outfit hanging from a metal hanger. The people at Ray's certainly have a quirky sense of humor.
- After dinner, drive east (right) on Main Street to the interstate. Go under the overpass until the pavement turns to gravel and then turn left. Drive for a little over a mile to a bluff overlooking the highway and with panoramic views in every direction. You should try and time this drive to coincide with sunset, so you can take in the radiant sun glow ridges and a world of brown rock that seems to go on forever. There are no houses or signs of anything other than a flashing cell tower that looks kind of cool in the evening light. You are on federal BLM land, which

means that you can pretty much go wherever you like and do whatever we want to do. Look for the edge of a slickrock bowl on the right, overlooking a dry wash, facing the setting sun. Then pull out your lawn chairs and your cooler of beer and proceed to watch the light show. The **Milky Way** will soon make its grand entrance. Use the **Star Chart** app on your cellphone to figure out the constellations. In the spring, summer, and fall there is always a **Meteor Shower** underway and you will find yourself squealing like a little kid whenever one cuts the heavens. Every once in a while, you will spot a **satellite**. It is truly invigorating to be back in the Southwest where the night sky is not polluted by light and you can see our little piece of the universe in all its splendor.

Best Hikes

- **The Wedge Rim Trail** - There is no formal trail, but rather, a gravel road running out to monumental vistas to the left and the right of the main overlook area by the entrance road. If you hike to both ends of the plateau you will cover a little over three miles of flat, easy walking with incredible views.
- **San Rafael River Trail** - When you get to the bridge park your car in one of the campsites or pull outs near the bridge. Then walk back to the bridge and look for a trail on the left that follows the San Rafael. You can go upstream or down. I always go downstream (right) because the canyon is narrower. This trail is easy to follow but a bit brushy. There is no end point. Just walk for a mile or so and then turn around and return to your car.

Insider Tips

- Don't make the mistake of frolicking in the muddy San Rafael River. You may be hot, and the water looks inviting, but when you dry off, you will feel like a mud monster as the mud dries on your skin.
- Tour buses have become the lifeblood of the small Mormon towns which have grown dependent upon the holy tourist dollar. The local Mormons and Navajos survive on seasonal tourism

and their winters are long and lonely. **So, try and spend a few bucks in each town you pass through so the hardworking people who service these stark and magical lands can survive too**.

Save Money!

- Before you leave the **Utah State University Eastern Prehistoric Museum** in Price, pick up the **FREE! park maps**, especially for the areas where you will be traveling next.
- On-street parking everywhere in Price is **FREE!**
- Download one of the many **FREE!** Star chart apps onto your cell phone so you can use it to see what you are looking at in the night sky. This is a great way to learn the constellations.
- Many of the Mormon towns, large and small, have weekly Farmers Markets, offering fresh local produce at an excellent price.

Day Five

ARCHES NATIONAL PARK

Arches can be a very hot place in spring, summer, and fall with very little shade, so you will need to make sure that you arrive at Arches National Park by nine and drive directly to the Delicate Arch trailhead. The Park Service has expanded the trailhead parking at Delicate Arch several times over the years, but it will never be big enough and usually fills by ten, so it's best to get an early start.

Delicate Arch is Utah's most iconic natural feature. It's featured on their license plates! And it is by far the most popular destination in the park. So, you should fully expect to encounter a mob scene and a human train all along the 1.5-mile-long trail (3 miles round trip), no matter what time you hike the trail. Sunset, while undoubtedly the best time to view Delicate Arch, is crazy busy. You will feel like you are in the Army and marching in a parade. So, avoid the temptation to do the sunset hike unless you don't mind really big crowds.

Upon arriving at the crowded Delicate Arch trailhead there will be tour buses and large school groups in the parking lot and many people waiting to use the bathrooms. The trash cans are often overflowing, and it has the feel of a sporting event or a rock concert.

So, get there early!

Utah is world-renowned for its many well-preserved fossils that were deposited millions of years ago in what were once ancient sea beds. This part of America and most of the Canyonlands were transformed from oceans, to lakes, to rivers and swamps many times over. Every rock formation you will pass through during your trip started as a sand dune or the bottom of some large body of water. Then

they were uplifted into their current position when the continental tectonic plates smashed into one another. Wind, water, and erosion have done the rest.

After visiting Arches National Park, you will venture into the happening town of Moab, known the world over as the *mountain bike capital of the world*. Moab has always marched to a different beat, first as a uranium town, the film center for Western movies, and then in the 70s as the home of the counterculture hippies. Today it resembles a commercial for Patagonia outdoor hedonism. It's essentially a redrock playground. So, make sure you take the time to roam the streets, check out the weird mix of stores and eateries, and talk to some of the friendly locals.

There is no place in Utah quite like Moab!

How to Get There

- Drive I-70 East to the exit for US 191 South. (16.7 miles)
  The speed limit is 80!
- Turn right onto **US 191 South** to the Arches Entrance Road on the left which is about 4 miles east of Moab. (27 miles)
  http://www.discovermoab.com/

Where to Stay

- **Super 8 Motel** in Moab, Utah
  https://www.wyndhamhotels.com/super-8/moab-utah/super-8-moab/overview?CID=LC:SE::GGL:RIO:National:02856&iata=00065402
- You will find all the chain motels in Moab. It's a big regional town. So, you should be able to easily book a room online.

Camping

- **Fee-based campgrounds on UT 128 along the Colorado River**. To avoid the hideous **Canyonlands by Night**, the boat and truck sound and light show that runs up the canyon

at sunset, you should avoid the lower camps, like where I used to stay at **Goose Island**, and camp instead at **Big Bend Campground** which is 7 miles up-canyon. Or you can camp at **Lower** or **Upper Drinks Campground** which are just before Big Bend.
http://www.discovermoab.com/campgrounds_park.htm

- The Bureau of Land Management is getting much more restrictive about primitive camping around Moab, so you should stick to the **fee-based campgrounds** along the Colorado River on **UT 128**.

Where to Eat

- Breakfast - You will need to get on the road by **7:30AM**, so eat the **FREE!** continental breakfast at the **Motel 6** in Green River, Utah.
- Lunch - Snacks. You will be in Arches National Park from morning until late afternoon and there is no place in the park to get lunch. You might want to stop at Subway or one of the sandwich places in Green River, Utah before you leave for Arches and pack a lunch in your cooler, so you can picnic in the National Park.
- Dinner - **Zax** has the biggest beer selection in town and they serve **gorgeous** pizza. I know that's a weird word to use for a pizza but check it out. It really is. They offer a great all-you-can-eat pizza bar and their upstairs patio deck is an amazing place to dine.
http://www.zaxmoab.com/

Best Things to Do

- Eat breakfast and check out of your hotel by **8AM**.
- Drive to Arches National Park
https://www.nps.gov/arch/index.htm

On your way into the park, stop for five minutes at the Visitor Center (you will return for a longer visit at the end of the day) and pick up the **FREE!**

park map. **If they give you a park map at the entrance station, then don't stop at the Visitor Center.**

- Hike to Delicate Arch
  https://www.nps.gov/arch/planyourvisit/delicate-arch.htm
- After your hike to Delicate Arch, drive to the **Devil's Garden** at end of the park road, a winding ribbon of asphalt that is lined with non-stop, eye-popping pinnacles and arches of red sandstone formations rising into the sky. The story of Arches is a complex tale of many chapters filled with long-extinct oceans, sand dunes, salty inland seas, coastal plains, braided river systems, and swamps. The underground salt dome created by the evaporating ocean that covered the area over 300 million years ago eventually punched its way to the surface and when it did, it cracked the sandstone above like the surface of freshly-baked loaf of bread which then eroded into all sorts of weird ridge lines, including arches of all shapes and sizes. Stop at several of the new pullouts to soak in the beauty and take some pictures. There are also short side roads that lead to scenic overlooks and quick hikes. Arches National Park has **more arches than any place else on earth – at last count there were over 2,000**. And they are continuously finding more!
- The **Devil's Garden loop trail is 7.8 miles long** and takes several hours. It has a few steep grades, the sun exposure is intense, and there are some short stretches of soft sand that are not fun to walk through. And after hiking Delicate Arch you are undoubtedly going to be tired. If it's hot (which it probably will be), it's best not to toy with heat exhaustion. So, you might want to dial it back by only hiking about a mile (2 miles round trip) out to **Landscape Arch**, the **fifth largest arch in the world and the longest in Arches National Park**. This first mile section is flat and an easy walking. **Double O Arch** is just a little bit farther past Landscape Arch but the trail climbs steeply up a sandstone ridge with narrow ledges and steep drop-offs with no shade. But you can still check it out from a vantage point near

Landscape Arch and then call it a day. On the way back, take the short spur trails to **Tunnel Arch** and **Pine Tree Arch**. ***https://www.alltrails.com/trail/us/utah/devils-garden-loop-trail-with-7-arches***

- After returning to the trailhead, drive leisurely back to the park entrance, stopping at several interesting attractions you missed on our way out, like **Sand Dune Arch**, **Fiery Furnace Viewpoint, Panorama Point, Balanced Rock, and Petrified Dunes Viewpoint**.
- Spend at least an hour at the truly exceptional **Visitor Center** where they offer a very informative short film about the park's weird geology, colorful exhibits about the history of the park and Grand County, a goofy sculpture of Delicate Arch, and a huge gift shop where you can some neat trinkets for friends and family.
- Check into your motel and go for a swim.
- Dine on **Zax's** lovely patio that has, like most of the outdoor dining places in town, misters to cool you down. It is the perfect way to end your day of fun and exploration in Arches, and to begin your extended visit to trippy Moab.
- After dinner, explore the interesting and eclectic mix of stores along **Main Street**.

Best Hikes

- **Delicate Arch** - This is the premiere hike in the park. The trail runs across open slickrock with no shade. The first half-mile is a well-defined trail. Follow the rock cairns. There are some interesting stops at the beginning of the trek, like an **old homestead** where some crazy rancher once carved out a surreal existence within the rocky inferno. And there is a nice **rock art panel** tucked into an **Entrada Sandstone** wall where desert-dwelling Indians carved pictures of people on horses and bighorn sheep. The trail climbs steadily (480') and then levels off near the arch. The Park Service has recently rerouted to avoid the fragile, black-crusted **cryptogamic soils** that are some of the oldest life forms on earth. Don't walk on the crusty soil! You should expect to find many people sitting and standing around the rim of the white and red sandstone bowl where Delicate Arch is majestically perched. Hikers wait patiently in line to get their picture snapped while standing under the massive arch. There is a shady spot to the left of the arch where you can sit and just watch the amusing parade of people. It is sort of like being in a great cathedral. People speak in whispers and even the kids are quiet and respectful. The sacred things in life are not always man made. Plan to spend about three hours hiking up and back to Delicate Arch. (3 miles round-trip - 3 hours)

- **Devil's Garden Loop Trail** - This trail will take you to **eight** of the premiere arches in the park. It is a strenuous hike along a well-maintained trail. But don't expect to be alone. This is also a very popular trail! Basically, the main trail loops around the desert with short spur trails to the arches. The first arch is **Tunnel Arch.** The second is **Pine Tree Arch**. The third, **Landscape Arch**, is a whopping 306-feet-long monster and is one of the largest in the world. At this point you will do some climbing, first to **Wall Arch**, and then a short steep climb up to **Navajo** and **Partition Arches**. Partition Arch offers some grand, sweeping views of the high desert and is probably going to be your stopping point. But if you still haven't had enough, you can hike another 2.4 miles (roundtrip) out to **Double O Arch** and **Dark Angel Arch**. Turn around and retrace your path back to the trailhead. (7.8 miles - 5 hours)

Insider Tips

- The park is undergoing a **multi-year construction project on the 18-mile main road** through the park that involves some widening and the installation of numerous pullouts and drainage features. They don't work on Saturdays and Sunday, so you should **plan your trip, so you are there on a weekend**. And you should check the **park website** before your trip to learn about the current conditions and if there any closures. ***https://www.nps.gov/arch/planyourvisit/conditions.htm***

- The Devil's Loop trail is crowded and some of the arches may be mobbed when you get there. Given that you will be retracing your route, you can just keep walking and stop at the arch on your way back, with the hopes that it won't be so busy.
- You can't swing a cat in Moab without hitting a pretty good restaurant. The best restaurants on websites like Trip Advisor will steer you to the places that are super expensive and fancy-schmancy. But here's what you do when you don't know where to eat: **ask a local**. It works well every time. And it's fun to talk to the people who live in the town you are visiting. You will invariably learn a lot and make new friends.
- There are several good **groceries** along **Main Street** (south side of town) and you will want to stock up on snacks and other items that you can put in your cooler for the days when there is no place to eat lunch. The **City Market** is going to be your best bet, with the cheapest prices and the widest selection. ***https://www.citymarket.com/stores/details/620/00410?cid=loc62000410_gmb***
- There is a **State Liquor Store** and you will want to stop in and stock up on **real** booze for your stay. Remember that the **beer in the groceries is only 3.2%.** ***https://abc.utah.gov/stores/index.html?storeNum=27***
- There are many good **outdoor outfitters** in Moab and it is a great place to buy or replenish your camping gear and supplies.
- The **Moab Adventure Center** on Main Street offers hummer safaris, mountain biking, tours of Arches National Park, zipline and ropes, flights and horseback rides, hot air balloon rides, jet boat tours, and jeep rentals. www.moabadventurecenter.com
- "Moab, Utah, well known for its spectacular mountain biking, also boasts some of the best road biking in the West. With the recent completion of the Moab Canyon Pathway, connecting Moab to two national parks and one state park, there are now over one hundred miles of paved non-motorized trails through absolutely amazing scenery. Moab Canyon pathway is not just

a bike lane on the side of the highway, but a path that allows riders/users to avoid the busy four-lane Highway 191 and have safe access to the state and national parks.

- The path begins at the pedestrian/bike bridge that crosses the Colorado River on Highway 128, just north of Moab. The super smooth blacktop snakes through 2 miles of the red rock canyon to the entrance of Arches National Park where you can exit for a 30-40 mile out and back ride, depending on your route choice inside the park.
- The path continues past Arches National Park for another 6.5 miles, and 525 vertical feet of climbing, crossing under Highway 191 to the beginning of Highway 313. The options here are to turn back for a scenic and speedy return from a short training ride, or to continue riding on Highway 313 for a challenging 24-mile climb to Dead Horse Point State Park or a 35-mile ride to Grand View Point in Canyonlands National Park's Island in the Sky. These mileages on Highway 313 are one way, so, with some figuring, riders can put together amazing century rides in some of the most beautiful country in the world!
- Mountain bikers and cyclocross riders will love the paved bike path as it gives direct access to the multiple trails at the Moab Brands Trail System (at mile 6) which adds a great warm-up on pavement to the trail and slickrock rides. From there, mountain bikers can access unlimited miles of dirt and slickrock routes including the Sovereign Trail, Bartlett Wash and Monitor & Merrimac areas.
- Not only bike riders will love this trail, but also hikers, runners, joggers and non-motorized vehicles of all sorts. Parents can pull their babies behind their bikes in trailers and all ages can enjoy the pathway, even if it is just for a leisurely stroll. Kids can try their new bikes on the flat sections on either end, since only the middle 4 miles have noticeable grade. It also provides a great place to hone your cross-country skiing skills during the off season with roller skies.

- Future plans for more paved bike paths include the Millsite Riverside Trail and a bike lane from the city of Moab to the Colorado River pedestrian bridge."
_http://www.discovermoab.com/moab_road_biking.htm_

Save Money!

- Before you leave the Arches National Park Visitor Center, pick up the **FREE! park maps**, especially for the areas where you will be traveling next.
- Parking is **FREE!** for an unlimited amount of time around Main Street.
- Visit some of the **FREE!** Art galleries in Moab.

Day Six

COLORADO RIVER TRIP

You will begin your sixth day by eating breakfast in Moab's first jail.

After a tasty breakfast, you will visit one of the truly unique roadside attractions in the Southwest, the Moab Rock Shop, run by a Moab legend who has filled his zany business with the craziest assortment of rocks and weird rustic art under the sun.

Then it's time to hit the river. There is nothing better than a fun river trip to lighten up your day, and you are going to glide down the Colorado River in a five-person raft with one of the oldest and best river companies in the Southwest.

You will run a very tame and beautiful section of the Colorado, go for a refreshing swim, and maybe even spot some Desert Bighorn Sheep. Your boatman will serenade you with wild stories and fun facts about the wondrous world passing by your little rubber raft.

After your fun and exciting afternoon on the river, it's time for a little stroll through the back streets of Moab before an early dinner.

After a fantastic dinner, you will follow the Colorado River, retracing your river trip, along one of America's most Scenic Highways, to a towering rock formation that will turn crimson in the setting sun.

And you will end your incredible day with a star show the likes of which you have never seen while surrounded by battleship mesas of pure delight.

Get ready for some wet dreams!

How to Get There

- Drive west on Main Street out of town and NAVTEC is located between W 200 North and West 400 North on the left.

After your river trip, if you still want to do a little hiking at the spectacular Fisher Towers:

- Drive west on Main Street out of town on US-191 N/N Main St.
- Turn right onto UT-191. (2.5 miles)
- Turn right onto UT-128 E. (21 miles)
- Turn right onto Fisher Towers Road. (2.2 miles)

Where to Eat

- Breakfast - **Jailhouse Cafe**, housed in the town's original jail. I always stop there when I'm passing through town. It's got it all: great location, congenial staff, fast service, and yummy eats. ***https://www.tripadvisor.com/Restaurant_Review-g60724-d677318-Reviews-Jailhouse_Cafe-Moab_Utah.html***
- Lunch - **NAVTEC** provides a box lunch.
- Dinner - The locals will tell you that one of the best places to eat in town is a place in the heart of town called **Arches Thai**. The decor is nothing special, but it has a nice vibe, the food is scrumptious, they have an excellent assortment of local micro-brews, and it is reasonably priced. They are closed on Tuesdays! I sampled one of the locally-brewed frosty beverages called **Dead Horse Amber** and it was out of this world. ***https://archesthai.com/***

Best Things to Do

- You don't need to get going early this morning. You can sleep until **8:30AM**, and then grab some breakfast at a leisurely pace.
- Finish eating breakfast on the back patio of the Jailhouse Cafe, one of Moab's most famous breakfast establishments, by **10AM**.

- Walk across Main Street to the Moab Information Center where they have many informative brochures about things to do in Moab. Pick up **FREE!** brochures and maps.
- Drive to the north end of town and check out the **Moab Rock Shop**, whose mercurial owner, **Lin Ottinger**, was one of the heroes in **Edward Abbey's** infamous novel **"The Monkey Wrench Gang"**. Inside and out, you will find an amazing assortment of mineral, gemstones, fossils, geologic maps, miners lanterns, Devil's claws, dinosaur bones, jewelry, lapidary, petrified wood, Indian pottery, old mining equipment, and indescribable works of art.
  http://www.moabrockshop.com/
- Drive over to **NAVTEC** at **11:30AM** and go for a Colorado River Trip with one of Moab's oldest and finest river running companies. This fun-filled half-day Colorado River raft trip is for the whole family. Each raft trip covers about seven river miles with fantastic scenery, informative guides, and moderate rapids. After checking in and signing the liability waivers, you will board a big passenger van around noon and cruise up **UT 128** which National Geographic rated the **second most scenic drive in America** (the Pacific Coast Highway is #1). The winding canyon road follows each bend in the river and for the first few miles there is a new **paved bike trail** at the river's edge that looks like big fun. The put-in for the river trip down the chilly Colorado is at **Rocky Rapid**. The river trip takes about **three hours**, and before you get on the river your two friendly guides will prepare a tasty lunch of cold cut sandwiches, veggies, fresh fruit, chips, cookies and lemonade in the shade of a riverside pavilion. About a mile downriver from the put-in you will pass the **Red Cliffs**, a working **dude ranch and winery**. They have about fifty tricked-out cabins nestled along the river and it would undoubtedly be a nice (but expensive) place to stay, except for the fact that you would have to drive back and forth to town all the time, and if you have been drinking that can get tricky. It does have a **FREE movie museum** and **$1 wine tastings** and that sounds pretty cool. Continuing down the river, your boatman will stop

in several of the calmer stretches of the river, so you can jump in for a refreshing swim before returning to Moab and your car. There are multiple outdoor companies offering essentially the same guided river trip, but NAVTEC was the original outfit in town and is still considered the best.
Rates: Adult: $54 | Youth: $44
Class: II- III **Length:** - Half-day 9am, 12pm, and 2pm
https://navtec.com/

- After the river trip, take a little stroll around the **Mill Creek area** on the east side of town. It's a great way to get away from the touron part of Moab and see how the locals live. The houses are mostly unpretentious, tidy, one-floor bungalows. The yards are well tended and many driveways sport ATV's and small boats. The historic homes, like the **Taylor House**, are made of faded red brick with wooden wrap-around porches.
- **Arthur Taylor House - Built 1894 - *"The Arthur Taylor House is an intact late 19th century farm complex with a two-story main house of brick. Its size and sophistication, in comparison with the crude homes of most of Moab's citizens, mark the importance of ranching in the area during the late 19th century. The Old Taylor Homestead is one of the few remaining historical and architectural assets of the town of Moab, which has suffered the baleful effects of uranium booms and tourist infestations."***
  - Adapted from the NRHP nomination submitted in 1980
  https://noehill.com/ut_grand/nat1980003908.asp
- Make sure you know what time **sunset** will take place and then be sure to finish your dinner and leave the restaurant **at least an hour before that time**. Drive back up the Colorado River Canyon on **UT 128**, the way they took you on the river trip earlier in the day, for about twenty miles and then head up the two-mile dusty gravel road to the **Fisher Towers** (there is a sign on the highway indicating the turn). Your mission is to arrive right on time, just as the sun is beginning to set and the towers are being day-glowed in wondrous red light. The whole

escarpment will be bathed in absolutely magical cathedral light that will literally throb with electric color.

- About a mile down the dirt road from the trailhead you will find a proper place to set up your lawn chairs, break out the beers, and await the arrival of the Milky Way. Perhaps **Jupiter** and **Venus** will already be shining in the sun's fading glow while **Saturn** comes up fast on the inside. Just point your phone app at the brightest stars and practice your constellations.

Best Hikes

- **Fisher Tower Trail** is a 3.9-mile trail that gets moderate traffic. It's an out and back trail located near Moab. You will hike on an easy to follow trail, past rock art and enormous red sandstone pinnacles. The last major tower at the 1.5-mile mark is called **The Titan**. The trail then heads out onto a spectacular ridge with majestic views of the towers.
  https://www.alltrails.com/trail/us/utah/fisher-towers-trail

Insider Tips

- **Red Cliffs** (you passed it on your river trip) is known as **John Ford Country** and it was **the** place for movie people to stay when filming movies like Ford's "Wagon Master", "Rio Grande", and "Stagecoach", to name but a few. And there have been many modern-day movies filmed around Moab like "Indiana Jones – The Last Crusade", "The Lone Ranger", "City Slickers", "Vanishing Point", and "Thelma & Louise". And virtually every river crossing you've seen in a western movie was the Colorado River in **Professor Valley**, where you will be rafting.
- The non-native **Eurasian Tamarisk** has taken over the river banks and squeezed out the native vegetation. This is a major problem on every river in the Southwest, especially the Colorado River, because a large tamarisk bush sucks about 200 gallons of water a day and it is estimated that they collectively drain **20 percent** of the Colorado River each year.
- The highlight of any river trip is spotting **Desert Bighorn Sheep** and there are many of them on the stretch of the Colorado River

that you will be running. They often come down to the river for a little drink, but they are hard to spot. So, keep a sharp eye out!

- At the takeout they will give you about fifteen minutes to swim before you pile back into the van for the ride back to town.
- At the junction of UT 128 and UT 191, there is **Matrimony Spring**. It is where Mormon kids in town went to fetch water and had romantic trysts which precipitated shotgun weddings eight months later. They say that if you drink from the spring with the one you love, you will soon be married; and if you drink alone, you will forever be wedded to the Canyonlands.
- Most of the motels in Moab (and most towns) have self-service laundries. If you want to wash your clothes, stop at the **Wells Fargo bank** on Main Street and pick up a roll of quarters so you can do your laundry.

Save Money!

- The **Moab Rock Shop** is **FREE!**
- Before you leave the Moab Visitor Center, pick up the **FREE! park maps**, especially for the areas where you will be traveling next.
- The **Film Museum at Red Cliffs** on UT 128 is **FREE!** You probably won't be able to do it this day, but it's something to file for one of the upcoming days you are in Moab and looking for interesting things to do.
- While you are at the Visitor Center, ask about the **FREE! Jurassic Walks and Talks**, where you can join a BLM paleontologist and explore the world of dinosaurs. Every weekend, through the summer, a BLM dinosaur expert will lead tours of dinosaur fossils and track sites in the Moab Area, beginning at the **Moab Information Center** on Main Street. ***https://www.blm.gov/press-release/blm-invites-public-free-jurassic-walks-and-talks-near-moab-utah***
- Parking at **NAVTEC** is limited but there is **FREE!** on-street and side street parking nearby.

Day Seven

CANYONLANDS NATIONAL PARK
ISLAND IN THE SKY

You will begin your day with a splash of pioneer and movie-making history at Moab's finest museum.

And then it's off to one of America's most enticing parks. Many of the folks who visit the Moab area stop at Arches and then move on to the other spectacular attractions in the area. Lord knows there is plenty to see. So, Canyonlands National Park is rarely very crowded, and the pace is relaxed. Canyonlands is comprised of two distinct areas, a magnificent mesa in the clouds called Island in the Sky, and a dazzling pincushion of sandstone pinnacles called The Needles.

Though separated by 120 road miles, you can see The Needles (where you will be going tomorrow) from a spectacular viewpoint at Island in the Sky. And when you visit the Needles you will be able to look back up to the north and see the Island in the Sky.

You will hike several short trails in the park, each completely different, and none of them very difficult. And you will stop at vistas that offer jaw-dropping views that seem like landscapes painted by the world's greatest grandmaster.

On your way back to Moab you will visit a grand viewpoint renowned the world over for its sensational sunsets.

And you will end your day eating dinner in Moab's only brewery where the locals go to eat and play.

So, get ready for some big fun!

How to Get There

- Drive north on US 191. (11 miles)
- Turn left onto UT 313. (15 miles)
- Continue straight on Grand View Point Road/Island in the Sky Road. (13 miles)
- Turn right on Upheaval Dome Road to the park entrance. (1.4 miles)

After checking out Canyonlands head over to Dead Horse State Park for a spectacular sunset view from the overlook:

- Backtrack the way you came into the park, heading east on Grand View Point Road. (14 miles)
- Turn right on UT 313 to Dead Horse State Park which is signed. (4 miles)

Where to Eat

- Breakfast - **Peace Tree Cafe**. They stamp their Sandwiches with a branded peace sign. ***http://www.peacetreecafe.com/***
- Lunch - You pick
- Dinner - **Moab Brewery** ***http://www.themoabbrewery.com/***

Best Things to Do

- Finish breakfast by **9AM**, and then it's time to check out some more of the town center, starting with the **Museum of Moab**, just a block away from the **Information Center** on Main Street. Walk up the airport runway-wide **E Center Street**, to a small and rather bland brick museum on the right, sitting across from the stately **Grand County Office Building**.
- The **Moab Museum** is a fun and informative place to explore during the heat of the day, or after a morning hike. It's run by a charming hippie lady named **Barbara Jackson** who only

charges **$5** for an experience that is priceless. Barbara has small rooms that showcase: paleontology, archaeology, geology, uranium mining, Anglo and Indian artifacts, the Civilian Conservation Corps camps in the area, adventure tourism, the Sagebrush Rebellion versus Ecodefenders, historic photos, a 1928 player piano, big cattle companies, the 1881 "Pinhook Battle" up in Castle Valley fought between the local Utes and several ranchers, the Old Spanish Trail, and the storied history of movie making in Professor Valley. Be sure to watch the captivating twenty-minute film about the actors and players who filmed many of the old Westerns around Moab. On the second floor you will find some fine Southwest photos; an outstanding assortment of polished stones in red velvet display cases; the first doctor's office run by Dr. JW Williams ($150 a year) who also sold drugs, books, stationery, Navajo baskets, wagons and buggies; and a very detailed re-creation of what the inside of a house in Moab would have looked like in the early 1900's. ***http://www.moabmuseum.org/***

- Drive to Canyonlands National Park - Island in the Sky. As always, your first stop in the **Canyonlands National Park** should be the **Visitor Center**. The one at Canyonlands is not up to snuff in relation to many other national parks, like nearby Arches, but they have a short movie that does a nice job of explaining the park's history and geology, and there is an okay gift shop. It is worth the 45-minute stop. And they have air conditioning! ***https://www.nps.gov/cany/index.htm***
- After the Visitor Center, begin your hiking day at the south end where there is an excellent viewpoint overlooking **The Needles** section of the park to the south that you will be visiting the next day. And there is an excellent **rim trail** that begins at the Overlook and offers mega-views of the Green River. After checking out the South Rim, slowly work your way back up the main road, doing several short hikes in different landscapes, thus getting a good cross-section of this magnificent park. (see best hikes below)

- On your way back from the park make a 4-mile detour to Dead Horse Point State Park where you can catch an amazing sunset. Check the precise time for sunset at the Canyonland National Park Service Visitor Center, so you can be right on time, along with many other sun worshipers. The park is open year-round from 6 a.m. - 10 p.m. There is a $15 entrance fee that is good for three days. The main viewpoint can be reached by car and is wheelchair accessible. They offer 8 miles of hiking trails and 17 miles of mountain bike trails that lead to spectacular overlooks. And they have a 21-unit campground that is open all year with electricity, a sanitary disposal station, and nice restrooms. They also have yurts to rent by reservation. This is a very popular place to watch the sun go down while the Canyonlands and the horseshoe bend in the Colorado River turns neon red. And there is, of course, a legend surrounding the place. In the 1800s, cowboys used to catch wild horses by driving the stallions and their mares toward the edge of the cliff and then use the 30-yard-wide point as a horse trap. The narrow neck of the rim was a natural corral. According to the legend, a band of horses were left corralled at the end of the dry point where they died of thirst within view of the Colorado River 2,000 feet below. This is also the spot where Thelma and Louise jumped their blue1966 Thunderbird. ***https://stateparks.utah.gov/parks/dead-horse/***
- Drive back to Moab and then go to dinner at the **Moab Brewery** on the south end of Main Street. The Moab Brewery is a classic local favorite. The food isn't anything special, but they have all the Utah microbrews, including almost every IPA brewed in the West. This is where the Moabites go to eat and drink and there are very few tourons. It is a cavernous building resembling a warehouse with high ceilings from which they hang boats and bikes. They even have several tricked-out jeeps with dummy drivers scattered around the dining tables. It's a unique Southwest hangout and a must see when visiting crazy Moab.
- This is going to be your last night in Moab and if you are still looking for some entertainment you can check out some live

country/western/rock music at the **Blu Pig** which is the **only place in town offering live music seven days a week.** ***http://www.blupigbbq.com/***

- If you are too tired to party after yet another action-packed day, then just head back to the hotel and sit in the hot tub, drinking boat drinks and watching the star show on the sky tube instead. A person can only have so much fun.

Best Hikes

- There are quite a few really good hikes in Island in the Sky but you will not have time to do them all. And some of them are strenuous and quite difficult. **As always, your first stop should be at the Visitor Center.** I would recommend that you begin your hiking day at the south end of the park. There is an excellent viewpoint where you can see The Needles section of the park that you will be visiting tomorrow. There is an exhilarating rim trail that begins at the Overlook and will offer views of the Green River. After exploring the South Rim, you can work your way back, checking out different areas by doing several short hikes, thus getting a good cross-section of this magnificent park. The park trails are works of art, some of the finest in America, and undoubtedly the work of a real artisan. They have these huge sandstone block cairns and beautiful chiseled steps through the slickrock.
https://www.nps.gov/cany/planyourvisit/hiking.htm
- **Grand View Point** - Easy walking along the canyon edge to the end of Island in the Sky Mesa with Panoramic views. Below the rim, you can see segments of the 100-mile **White Rim Road** looping around and below the Island in the Sky mesa top. Four-wheel-drive trips usually take two to three days, and mountain bike trips take three to four days. When the weather is dry, the White Rim Road is moderately difficult for high-clearance, four-wheel-drive vehicles. The steep, exposed sections of the **Shafer Trail, Lathrop Canyon Road, Murphy's Hogback, Hardscrabble Hill, and the Mineral Bottom** switchbacks make the White Rim loop a challenging mountain bike ride and

require extreme caution for both vehicles and bikes during periods of bad weather. From your lofty perch in the sky, a lone jeep creeping slowly along the tiny buff ribbon of dirt road below looks like the Mars Rover. (2 miles - 1.5 hours)

- **Mesa Arch** - Easy walk to the arch at the edge of the canyon. Great place to snap a photo. Check out the interpretive sign about fragile soils. And then notice the area around the sign and see how numerous hikers have ignored the warning and destroyed a thousand years of soil by their careless steps. (0.5 miles - 30 minutes)
- **White Rim Overlook** - Walk to an east-facing overlook for some breathtaking views of the Colorado River, Monument Basin, and the La Sal Mountains. Limited trailhead parking. (1.8 miles - 1.5 hours)
- **Whale Rock** - Short but somewhat steep walk up Whale Rock leads to views of Upheaval Dome and surrounding area. (1 mile - 1 hour)

Insider Tips

- Along meandering Mill Creek there is a lovely paved **greenway trail** lined by shady cottonwood trees that leads you past **Swanny City Park** where the **Farmers Market** is held on Fridays from 4-7.
- If there is one common denominator to the national parks in the Southwest, it is the **road construction**. The summer season is when they improve the roads, so no matter where you go, you should pretty much count on doing the "one lane ahead" dance which involves sitting in a long line of RV's and buses waiting for a pilot car to slowly come along and lead you through the work area. So, check the websites at each park to see if there is road construction. If there is, then you need to allow yourself some extra time for travel.
  https://www.nps.gov/cany/planyourvisit/road-conditions.htm

- The National Park Service will have the precise time for sunset posted in the Visitor Center at Canyonlands.
- **Trails:** Trails are marked with cairns (small rock piles). Please do not disturb cairns or build new ones. Signs are located at trailheads and intersections. All backcountry trails are primitive and rough. Water may be found in some canyons but is rarely available in others. All water should be purified before drinking. Spring and fall are the preferred times of year for hiking due to temperature and water availability.
- **Day Use Permits:** Traveling on four wheel-drive roads into Salt Creek, Horse and Lavender canyons by vehicle, bicycle or horse requires a day use permit. (See other side for permit information.)
- **Backcountry Permits:** All overnight stays, except those at Squaw Flat Campground, require a backcountry permit. Visitors are responsible for knowing and following backcountry regulations. (See other side for permit information.)
- **Pets:** Pets are only permitted on paved and two- wheel-drive roads. Pets are not allowed on trails or four-wheel drive roads (either inside or outside of a vehicle). Pets are permitted in your campsite at Squaw Flat Campground. Pets must be leashed at all times.
- **Cryptobiotic Soil Crusts:** An important feature of the Colorado Plateau is the black. knobby crust often seen growing on soil surfaces. Cryptobiotic soil holds moisture, prevents erosion and contributes nutrients to the desert environment. The crust is easily broken and crushed by tracks. Please do not step or drive on these living soils.

Safety Information: The high desert is a land of extremes. For a safe and enjoyable visit, please follow these guidelines:

- Drink a minimum of one gallon of water per day. Avoid overexposure to the intense sun.

- Spring, summer and fall temperatures may become extremely hot. Save strenuous activity for morning or evening hours.
- During winter, temperatures drop well below freezing. Wear warm wool or synthetic clothing. Carry storm gear and a flashlight.
- During lightning storms avoid lone trees, cliff edges and high ridges. Return to your vehicle if possible.
- Watch weather conditions. Slickrock lives up to its name when wet or icy!
- Remember that climbing up is easier than climbing down.
- Flash floods occur with amazing rapidity. When caught in flash flood conditions, go to high ground. Do not attempt to drive through washes in flood.
- Group members should stay together to avoid becoming lost.
- If you become lost, stay where you are. Make your location obvious to searchers.

Save Money!

- Before you leave the Canyonlands National Park Visitor Center, pick up the **FREE! park maps**, especially for the areas where you will be traveling next.

Day Eight

NEGRO BILL CANYON & CANYONLANDS NATIONAL PARK - THE NEEDLES

This is going to be an action-packed day, bookended by two of the best hikes in Canyonlands.

You will start your day early with a magical hike up a dazzling little creek to a massive desert-varnished-stained natural bridge that will glow like neon when the rising sun crests the mesa top and starts baking the wondrous canyon like a big loaf of bread.

Then it's back into Moab for one last meal at an amusing Mexican food truck.

After buying your last supplies in the *big* city, it's time to head south into the heart of Canyonlands, passing goofy roadside attractions, a keyhole arch, and one of the largest and most intricate rock art sites in the Southwest, before landing in the Needles section of Canyonlands National Park, where red sandstone pinnacles rise into the sky like a pincushion dream world.

You will hike across slickrock into a jumbled world of sandstone rocket ships that few people ever see. And the viewpoint overlooks will take your breath away as you explore a landscape that seems to have been carved by the hand of god.

And you will end your day in a small Mormon farming town where time seems to stand still.

So, get ready to do some serious (and fun!) hiking!

How to Get There

- Turn onto US-191 N/N Main Street. (2.5 miles)
- Turn right onto UT-128 E. (3.1 miles)
- Turn right to the trailhead.

When you are ready to leave Moab, and continue your journey:

- Drive US 191 South out of Moab (40 miles)
- Turn right onto UT 211 West (29 miles)
- Turn right onto Lock Hart Road (4.3 miles)
- Turn left to stay on Lock Hart Road to Visitor Center (3.6 miles)

After your visit to The Needles:

- Backtrack the way you came in until you get to US 191 (37 miles)
- Turn right on US 191 South to Monticello (15 miles) ***https://en.wikipedia.org/wiki/Monticello,_Utah***

Where to Stay

- **Inn at the Canyons** in Monticello, Utah (indoor pool) ***http://www.monticellocanyonlandsinn.com/***

Camping

- **Mountain View RV Park and Campground** in Monticello, Utah ***https://mountainviewutah.com/***
- The nearest public land where you can camp for **FREE!** is located on the Forest Service land. Take W 200 S out of Monticello. Bear left and the road turns into Abajo Drive. Keep bearing left and the road turns into N Creek (101) and drive a few miles on a gravel road until you see the large brown sign marking National Forest land. Take any dirt road and camp or continue to the **Dalton Spring Campground** at the base of the **Abajo Mountains** run by the Forest Service.

https://www.fs.usda.gov/recarea/mantilasal/recarea/?recid=73250

Where to Eat

- Breakfast - You need to get an early start, so eat the **FREE!** Continental breakfast at the hotel.
- Lunch - **Quesadilla Mobilla** in Moab. Quesadilla Mobilla is located in a food truck. I'm not sure why, but food trucks are quite popular in Moab. And while they are each housed in a colorful truck, the trucks never move. Quesadilla Mobilla has picnic tables under cottonwood shade trees and is just a funky outdoor cafe. It's pretty hard to screw up Mexican food. It's equally hard to stand out. Quesadilla Mobilla serves some of the best Mexican food under the sun. The portions are huge, and the spices are lively. And you can get a great lunch for about $10. ***https://www.quesadillamobilla.com/***
- Dinner - **Line Camp Steakhouse** just north of Monticello, Utah ***https://www.tripadvisor.com/Restaurant_Review-g57071-d1783944-Reviews-Line_Camp_Steakhouse-Monticello_Utah.html***

Best Things to Do

- Eat an early breakfast at the Motel, or **Denny's** right next door, and be on the road to the Grandstaff Trailhead by **6:45AM**.
- Begin your hike up **Negro Bill Canyon** at **7AM**. You want to beat the heat and catch the rising sun on **Morning Glory Natural Bridge**. When you see the light on this spectacular sandstone bridge, you will be glad you got an early start. ***http://www.discovermoab.com/family_nb.htm***
- Return to the motel and check out.
- Buy some fresh organic fruit from the friendly lady selling Colorado fruit from her pickup by the right side of the road just down the road from the Super 8.
- Eat lunch at the **Quesadilla Mobilla** food truck in the middle of town.

- Pick up your snacks, ice, gas, liquor and any other supplies you will need before leaving Moab. **This is the last big town you will be in for the rest of the trip!**
- As you are driving down US 191 toward The Needles you will come to the enchanting **Wilson Arch** (91 feet long by 46 feet high) nestled in a cliff face to the left of the highway. Stop at the wide pull out and then follow a short, easy trail up to the base of the impressive rock window.
https://en.wikipedia.org/wiki/Wilson_Arch
- Forty miles south of Moab, turn off US 191 and head west on **UT 211** for twelve miles **(do not take the first right turn off the highway for The Needles!**) until you come to one of the most outstanding rock art panels in America: **Newspaper Rock State Historic Monument**. There are over **650 distinct petroglyphs** chiseled into the black stained **desert varnish** of a **Wingate Sandstone** cliff face that marks the beginning of **Indian Creek Canyon**. This valley between the mesas has been a major travel way for Indians for the past 2,000 years. The rock face is covered with pictures of humans, animals, and strange symbols. The later images depict men hunting on horses.
And there is even what I can only describe as one of the **first Indian cartoons**, featuring a horseman shooting an arrow at a deer and the deer is shitting itself in fear. Rock art experts have debated the meaning of every little picture and why there are so many figures on this one sandstone panel. I'm no expert, but my guess is that lots of people passed that way over the years and the mural was close to the trail and easy to draw upon. But in the end, it remains a cultural mystery because there's no one living who can explain its original intent.
https://en.wikipedia.org/wiki/Newspaper_Rock_State_Historic_Monument
- It is another 17 miles to the entrance of the **Needles**, and along the way you will pass through the lushly irrigated **Indian Creek Valley** where several huge ranches spread across the land like a green carpet of wheat and alfalfa dotted with munching horses and cows.

- Make a brief stop at the **Canyonlands Visitor Center** to check out the local conditions and look at the displays and trinkets for sale. The VC is very tiny and there's not much to look at, so this should be a quick stop. But before you leave, talk to the ranger and have them show you on the park trail map exactly the route to the **Chesler Park Viewpoint.**
  https://www.nps.gov/cany/planyourvisit/needles.htm
- Drive to the **Elephant Hill trailhead** and hike out to the **Chesler Park Viewpoint**.
  http://www.moab-utah.com/trails/needlestrails.html
- On your way out of the park, stop at the pullouts along the entrance road to check out **Wooden Shoe Butte** and then do the short hike to **Roadside Ruin**.
- Drive back to **US 191** past Newspaper Rock and turn south (right.)
- Check into your motel, go for a swim, and then eat a delicious dinner in Monticello at a Wild West steakhouse.

Best Hikes

- **Negro Bill Canyon Trail** - This is a 4.3 mile (2.5 hours), out and back, lightly-used trail near Moab that runs along a meandering creek and is rated as moderate. The hike ends at Morning Glory Natural Bridge which is only separated from the cliff by about 15'. It is the 5th largest span in the world! You should try your best to arrive at the trailhead a little after seven. By getting an early start, you will beat the heat and have the lovely canyon to yourself. The air smells cool and sweet and the entire canyon will still be in full shade. The trail runs along a very lovely shallow little stream that will tinkle and sing to you the whole way. There are lots of shady places to chill as the canyon wrens practice their morning songs. There are over ten stream crossings and **you are going to get your feet wet** eventually so you might as well just bite the bullet and get your shoes wet at the first crossing. That way you won't worry about it anymore and you can just enjoy the hike. There is **Poison Ivy** along the sides of the trail in some of the wet spots. There is even a photo sign at the trailhead warning people who don't know what it looks like. It doesn't grow over the trail, so there is no reason for a hiker to ever come in contact with it. I guess the BLM just want people to be aware that it is there. If you followed these directions and got on the trail early, you will arrive at **Morning Glory Natural Bridge** just before the sun comes breaking over the rim. The sandstone bridge is almost black against the blue sky of morning. Take a few minutes to sit on some large flat stones by a rainbow seep that trickles down the psychedelic wall at the head of the canyon and it feels a bit like you are attending early morning mass. And when the sunlight hits the desert varnish-stained sandstone the whole bridge comes alive in glorious color. Desert varnish is a blackish manganese-iron deposit that gradually forms on exposed sandstone cliff faces because of weathering and bacteria. Standing directly under the massive natural bridge, which is only separated from the rim by a mere 15 feet, it looks like the leg of the world's biggest dinosaur. The hike back will be mostly in the sun, but it still won't be too hot, so it's all good. In fact, it is like doing a completely different hike because everything that had been in the shade on the way up will now be all lit up and shiny.

- I'm sure that you have been wondering about the name Negro Bill Canyon. In these times of political correctness, it has, of course, become embroiled in controversy. How did the canyon get such a curious name, you ask? William Grandstaff was a cowboy who was half African-American and half Indian. He hailed from Alabama and was one of the first settlers in the Moab area around 1877. He came with a buddy named Frenchie and they set up shop in the abandoned Elk Mountain Mission Fort where they scraped out a meager existence together. Frenchie soon moved on but Grandstaff stayed until 1881, farming, ranching, and prospecting. He built a cabin and two ice houses in the canyon that bears his name. In 1881, there was an infamous Indian uprising and Grandstaff was accused of selling whiskey to the Indians. He feared there would be repercussions. So, he quickly abandoned his cabin and forty head of cattle and told no one where he was going. He eventually popped up in Colorado and settled in Glenwood Springs where he became a respected member of the community until his death in 1901. Early settlers in Moab called the canyon Negro Bill Canyon for obvious reasons. Well, it was originally called "Nigger Bill Canyon", but after the first round of historical revision, it was softened to the more palatable "Negro". In 2017, the Moab City Council failed by one vote to change the name of Negro Bill Canyon. Interestingly, the NAACP opposed the name change. But the city did change the name of the trailhead parking lot to the Grandstaff Trailhead. No doubt because that's what the public sees from the highway. And before long, the offensive name will drift off into history and be forgotten ***https://www.alltrails.com/trail/us/utah/grandstaff-trail***

- **Chesler Park Viewpoint Trail** - From the trailhead, hike 1.5 miles to a trail junction where you will turn right. The first part of the hike wanders along slickrock benches. The middle part of the hike crosses a rugged red rock canyon and in another 0.6 miles (2.1-mile mark) you will come to the **Elephant Hill Trail junction** and you will turn right. Go 0.6 (2.7-mile mark) as the trail climbs a steep, rocky slope to a pass overlooking the Chesler Park. At the next trail junction go left for another 0.2 to the **Chesler Park Viewpoint**. Snap some photos, rest and drink some water, eat some snacks, and then return to your car the way you came. (5.8 miles round-trip - 3.5 hours) ***http://www.hikingwalking.com/destinations/ut/ut_se/canyonlands/chesler_park***

Insider Tips

- In the Southwest it's no big deal if you get your shoes wet because you can dry your shoes in the car quickly. The hot sun turns your car into an oven and quickly bakes them dry in a couple of hours.

Save Money!

- Before you leave the Visitor Center, pick up the **FREE! park map**, especially where you will be traveling next.
- Birdwatching is **FREE!** And the Canyonlands is packed with many interesting and colorful birds.
- Many of the Mormon towns stage local fairs and special events that are **FREE!** So, check at the **Visitor Centers** to see what's happening as you are passing through.
- Wilson Arch is **FREE!**

Day Nine

EDGE OF THE CEDARS, BLUFF, MEXICAN HAT & THE SAN JUAN RIVER

This is going to be a very busy day, packed with some wonderful attractions and loaded with Mormon pioneer history and fascinating Indian prehistory.

But there isn't going to be a lot of hiking. That's not to say that you won't be doing a fair amount of walking. At each of the stops, like at Fort Bluff, you will want to roam around, and there are short hikes to the Chacoan Great House, Sand Island and the petroglyphs, and the Mexican Hat.

But unlike the previous days, there will not be a long, tiring hike.

At this point, you could probably use a day off from hiking.

So, enjoy this sightseeing travel day and get ready for tomorrow which will have plenty of good hiking.

How to Get There

- Drive US 191 South out of Monticello to the town of Blanding Utah. (22 miles)

After stopping at the Edge of the Cedars in Blanding, head to Bluff, Utah:

- Drive south on US 191 to Bluff, Utah (26 miles)

After Bluff, Utah, head to Sand Island, Utah:

- Continue south on US 191 (4.2 miles)

- Turn left at the sign for Sand Island.

After Sand Island, Utah, head to Mexican Hat:

- Continue south on US 191. (0.8 miles)
- Continue straight on Us 163 South (18 miles)
- Look for the Mexican Hat rock formation on your left.
- Turn left onto an all-weather gravel road (County Road 2161) that will lead you to the Mexican Hat. (0.3 mile)

After Mexican Hat, head to the San Juan Trading Post:

- Continue south on UT 163 to the bridge over the San Juan River and your motel is on the right. (5 miles)

Where to Stay

- **San Juan Inn** in Mexican Hat, Utah. This historic hotel and trading post sits by the bridge over the San Juan River and feels like southern Mexico. It has a fine restaurant overlooking the muddy river and an exceptional **trading post** where you can buy genuine authentic **Navajo jewelry** for a reasonable price. ***http://www.sanjuaninn.net/***

Camping

- Sand Island Campground on US 191, a few miles past the junction with US 261. ***https://www.grandcanyontrust.org/sand-island-campground***
- Almost all the land between Sand Island and the San Juan Inn is managed by the BLM. Almost any gravel road on either side of the highway, including the one to Mexican Hat, is open for **FREE**! Primitive camping.

Where to Eat

- Breakfast - **Peace Tree Juice Café** in Monticello, Utah

https://www.tripadvisor.com/Restaurant_Review-g57071-d1654543-Reviews-Peace_Tree_Juice_Cafe-Monticello_Utah.html

- Lunch - **Twin Rocks Cafe** in Bluff, Utah. The **Twin Rocks Cafe** is tucked back into the base of an amazing rock formation on the north end of the tiny town of **Bluff** that sits along the banks of the muddy **San Juan River**. The restaurant is nestled in the shadow of the towering **Twin Rocks**. It is a must-see place to stop and eat. Do yourself a favor and order the wonderfully tasty **Navajo taco**.
  https://www.yelp.com/biwz/twin-rocks-cafe-bluff
- Dinner - **San Juan Inn** in Mexican Hat.

Best Things to Do

- Check out of your hotel by **8AM**.
- After breakfast, drive to the **Monticello Visitor Center** which is in the middle of town off Main Street (US 191). Attached to the center is the **FREE! Frontier Museum** where they showcase a very curious mix, starting with the standard private collections of **looted Indian artifacts** from Anasazi sites in the area, with the names of the pot hunters, like **Nell Dalton**, proudly displayed as generous benefactors; items like linens and dishes from the long-gone **Hyland Hotel**; a wooden chair from the **Home of Truth Chapel**; minerals, fossils, and monstrous **sharks teeth**; a **Champion Cowboy saddle**; a galvanized steel **ballot box**; **Ray Jarvis'** old tool collection; landline telephones and the town's first switchboard; a white oven/stove and **gas iron**; a **huge typewriter**; old dresses and a baby carriage; an **electric mangler** and all things cowboy; historic photos of cowboys and Indians; a very odd **doll collection**; medical equipment, including a **weird EKG machine**; a collection of **barbed wire**; cameras, radios, and a hodgepodge mix of unrelated items from local houses and businesses. One of the more interesting items in the Frontier Museum is the **Bull Durham Tobacco Quilt** that was made from old Bull Durham sacks by a local lady who collected them along the side of the road and from the local

cowboys who saved their sacks for her. When she had collected enough of them, she dyed them yellow and pink and made two lovely quilts. The quilter was following the pioneer creed: "Use It Up, Wear It Out, Make Do Or Do Without". But the strangest exhibit were items donated by the family of **Marie Ogden** of New Jersey, who came to San Juan County in 1933 after the death of her husband, with a group of about thirty followers who called themselves **The Home of Truth**. They were mostly disillusioned easterners who were fleeing the Great Depression and they were following Marie who had promised to lead them to the place of the **Second Coming of Jesús Christ**. Marie's followers believed she was the reincarnation of the **Virgin Mary**. Apparently, the local Mormons did not find these religious fanatics amusing and no one would sell them land around Monticello. But Marie was tenacious, and she built her mission by a creek near what is today the entrance to The Needles section of Canyonlands National Park. And then she bought the **San Juan Record** newspaper in 1934 and served as its editor until 1949, when she sold the paper. She also tried her hand at farming, mining, construction projects, and taught music. She died in a nursing home in **Blanding, Utah** in 1975, at the age of 91.
***http://utahsadventurefamily.
comfrontier-museum-in-monticello/***

- It will only take you about thirty minutes to check out the museum, and after that, spend a little time chatting with the local ladies who run the Visitor Center. They know all the town gossip. And the neatest thing in the whole place is **"Little Town"**, an amazing **diorama of Monticello between 1888-1911**.

- Walk outside to the adjacent barn next to the Visitor Center where you will find the ginormous 20-feet-long by ten-feet-wide by eleven-feet-high, 650 rpm, 22,725-pound, 4-cylinder gas tractor called the "**Big Four "30" - The Giant Horse"** made in 1913 by the **Emerson-Brantingham Company of Minneapolis**. It is a remnant of olden days when colossus machinery ruled the day. The initial cost of this behemoth that moved along at a top speed of 3 mph and needed a full-time maintenance crew, was $4,000, a hefty price indeed in those days for a little farming town in the middle of nowhere. But the local working wage per day was $11.20, and the total cost for using the Big Four tractor in grubbing and plowing was $3.51. So, it was a good deal – at least for a few years, until it started regularly breaking down. Eventually, they just dug a big hole out in the desert and buried the monstrosity.

- Drive to the **Edge of the Cedars** in Blanding, Utah. This is one of the best **Indian museums** in the world and it's worth spending at least two hours at this amazing place. The Edge is a scientific museum created and curated by reputable archaeologists who have gathered the museum's artifacts through painstaking and meticulous excavations, not display cases filled with locally looted items without provenance that you have found in all the little Utah museums from Green River to Monticello. You see, if you don't know exactly where an artifact came from – and I mean the exact layer of dirt where it was unearthed from – then all you have is a shiny thing. It's useless from a scientific standpoint, though on the black market, it might be worth a pretty penny.

  The Edge of the Cedars Museum is the real deal, complete with excellent storyboards that explain what you are looking at and what it all really means.

  That said, the archaeologists are still playing the "we used to think but now we know" game about many controversial Anasazi mysteries, like what the rock art symbols mean, and why the Anasazi completely abandoned their spectacular cities like **Chaco Canyon** and **Mesa Verde** by **1300**.

  I still think it was a combination of factors: prolonged drought and the water table dropping, thus making it hard to farm near their homes; depletion of natural resources like wood, forcing them to go further and further afield; competition and warfare;

and disease and poor nutrition. All these factors - and probably some others we don't know about - created the Perfect Storm.

And then there's the raging **Ancestral Puebloans controversy**. The experts can't even agree what the hell to call the ancient Indians who inhabited the American Southwest. On one side we have the old school archaeologists and anthropologists who have always used the term **Native-American**. In the 70s, that term went out of vogue and everyone started calling them ***Anasazi***, a term coined by the infamous cowboy pothunter **Richard Wetherill** in the 1880s, which is a Navajo word meaning **"ancient ancestor"** or **"ancient enemy"**, depending on who you talk to. And now, in the **Political Correctness Period**, the experts have coined the tongue-twisting phrase ***Ancestral Puebloans*** because each Pueblo group (Acoma, Cochita, Isleta, Jemez, Laguna, Nambe, Okhay, Picuris, Sandia, Santa Ana, Santa Clara, San Felipe, Taos, Zia, and Zuni) have their own names. For instance, the **Hopi** refer to their ancestors as the ***Hisatsinom.*** But the **Acoma** and the **Laguna** don't want to use a Hopi word. In the end, **we are all immigrants**. The ***Indians of America*** came across the land bridge from Siberia while others perhaps came by sea. They are not **indigenous people** (a truly ridiculous phrase concocted by pinhead academics trying to sound smart) or **Native-Americans**. DNA research has proven beyond a reasonable shadow of a doubt that we are **ALL** Africans. But the name African-Americans has already been taken for another race of people. ***Indians*** - a name coined by Columbus who thought he had landed in India when he came ashore in the Caribbean and encountered people living there - is certainly a stupid name. America obviously has nothing to do with India. But it's as good, or as dumb, a name as any. And the many Indians who have befriended me over the years don't care about the term one way or the other. They define themselves by their **tribe**.

The museum also tries to tackle the thorny issue of locals from the Blanding area systematically looting Anasazi sites for the past century. They unravel two very intriguing CSI stories of forensic investigation. The first involving a fellow who was cleverly captured by running a DNA test on the filter from a cigarette he had tossed in the backfill from a site he was looting called **House Rock Ruin**. The looter was prosecuted under the **Archaeological Resource Protection Act of 1979**. In the second case another looter was caught and convicted because of his habit of leaving his empty Mountain Dew cans. And once again, his DNA ultimately did him in. **It is estimated that 80 percent of Indian archaeological sites in America have been looted and more than 90 percent around Blanding.**

*** Check out my mystery novel "Anasazi Strip" to get a flavor for the pothunting of Anasazi sites on the Colorado Plateau.**

The museum also features one of the largest pottery collections in the world, along with baskets, ornaments, jewelry, blankets and clothing, ceremonial objects, architecture and masonry styles, weapons and hunting snares, toys and dolls, and miniature pottery items that were probably made by or for children.

The **Puebloan Pathways** exhibits are organized by time period, starting with the first American Indians, called **Paleo-Indians**, who followed the land bridge from Siberia after the last Ice Age.

This is called the **Archaic Period** and began 11,000 years ago. (6500 BC - 1200 BC)

The **Basketmaker II Period** ran from 1200 BC- 500 AD

The **Basketmaker III Period** ran from 500 AD - 750 AD

The **Puebloan I Period** ran from 750 AD - 900 AD

The **Puebloan II Period** ran from 900 AD - 1100 AD

The **Puebloan III Period** ran from 1100 AD - 1300 AD

The **Pueblo Historic Period** ran from 1600 - 1959

The museum also has some amazing **photos of Canyon Country**, taken by **famous Southwest photographers**.

There is also a fantastic exhibit featuring items that were found at the 850 AD **pueblo site** that was excavated where the Edge of the Cedars Museum is located today. This was the genesis for the creation of the museum. And the **Richards Perkins Collection** of ceremonial and utilitarian pottery in their black display cases is one of the best you will ever see.

- After viewing the inside exhibits walk back outside through the doors at the rear of the building to check out the restored **Pueblo**. They even have a sturdy wooden ladder that you can use to climb down into the restored **ceremonial Kiva**. There is also a very cool **sculpture garden** with a dancing flutist sporting a very prodigious prick. And there is a dreamy **sun sculpture** designed to pinpoint the winter and summer solstice.
- After roaming around the Kiva and sculpture garden, go back inside and peruse the extensive **Museum Store** with its excellent selection of books; jewelry; t-shirts; and Native-American crafts, like healing balms made from native plants and **Tewa Tees prayer flags**.
- One of the neatest things about this isolated and forgotten part of Utah is that many of the businesses are now staffed by Indians.
  https://stateparks.utah.gov/parks/edge-of-the-cedars/
- Eat lunch at the **Twin Rocks Cafe** in Bluff, Utah. You can charge your electronics right at your table and eat a yummy meal at this Indian-run restaurant.
- After cooling off at the Twin Rocks Cafe, drive down Main Street (US 191) to the super-duper **San Juan Co-Operative Company Visitor Center** right off US 191 in the middle of town. The cavernous, two floor historic building is the gateway to **Bluff Fort** which is **FREE!** This is worth exploring for the next hour. When you walk into the fort you will be immediately greeted by several friendly cowboy/cowgirl docents, many related to the first settlers, who will orient you and answer your questions.
  http://bluffutah.org/bluff-fort/

  Inside the fort there are fifteen replica **cottonwood log cabins** and each of the cabins are exactly the same, one room with a bed, fireplace, and a small table and chairs. There are signs and photos that tell the touching story of each family. Every cabin has been lovingly refurbished by their descendants. You gotta love those Mormons! There is also the **schoolhouse** that had no books at the start, the **blacksmith shop**, and the **church/meeting house**.

The fort was not really a fort but rather, a **stockade village**, with a wooden stake fence to corral the children and animals. All the cabins faced inward, showing that they were not concerned about being attacked. The Mormons made a genuine effort to live in peace with the Indians. The Navajos even referred to the Mormons by another word, ***Gáamalii***, to differentiate them from the average murdering white man who they called ***bilagáana.***

The fort also features a clever **water wheel** section where water runs continuously through the various wheels, troughs, and stone sluices, constantly recirculating like a MC Escher drawing.

Other attractions at Fort Bluff include the **Craft Center** where you can rent period costumes and snap goofy photos of yourself and your crew.

There is a spacious gift shop, bathrooms, ice cream, sodas and snacks, and a shady picnic area with tables and seats overlooking the interior of the fort. Fort Bluff is a great place to just chill a spell.

- The story of Fort Bluff is the hair-raising tale of the **San Juan Mission**, a death-defying leap of faith conducted by the devoted Mormon pioneers who blazed a trail through some of the roughest terrain in the world from Escalante to Bluff in 1879. ***https://en.wikipedia.org/wiki/San_Juan_Expedition***
- After your fun little visit to the Bluff Fort, drive along **3rd East Street** for a few blocks past an attractive assortment of sturdy homes, and at the end of the street turn left and follow the signs up the gravel road a short distance to the tidy **town cemetery** overlooking the *bustling metropolis* of Bluff. The grave stones include a sad line of little metal crosses, marking the last resting place of some indigent World War II veterans - probably Navajos.

- On your way back down from the cemetery there is a small kiosk on the left. Park and then follow a narrow path to the right, leading to the shattered ruins of a **Chacoan Great House**.
  http://www.gjhikes.com/2013/12/bluff-great-house.html
- On the west end of Bluff is the town's social hub, a convenience store and gas station called **K & C's Trading Post**, where you should fill up with gas, ice, and any other supplies you might need. The next services, other than the **San Juan Inn**, will not be until **Hanksville**, about 150 miles to the northwest, and Bluff will be less expensive.
  https://www.tripadvisor.com/Restaurant_Review-g56937-d5999601-Reviews-K_C_Trading_Post-Bluff_Utah.html
- A few miles southwest of Bluff along UT 191 is **Sand Island**. Before hitting the river, take the first right and follow the signs a short distance to the rather extensive, but badly vandalized, **petroglyph panels** along the shiny black, iron-stained sandstone walls to the right that are between **300 and 3,000 years old**. There's a lot going on with this rock art site, but it's hard to see. It's still definitely worth a 15-minute stop before heading down to the San Juan River. You will see a boat launch by the lazy river. This is the put-in for San Juan river trips and is often quite busy with people loading their boats. Feel free to get your feet wet and chill a bit. But the river runs muddy, so it's not a great place to swim because when you dry off you will feel like a mud monster._
  http://anasazihikes.com/Sand_Island.php
- Drive to the Mexican Hat right off US 163. (Can't miss it.) Mexican Hat is a large flat piece of sandstone sitting precariously upon a multi-tiered rock base on the top of a hill that looks like a Mexican Sombrero, hence the name. There is no town. There are no houses. You just follow a wide gravel road to a stupendous rock formation in an area of the country where erosion does some very strange things. There is a small town called **Mexican Hat** across the San Juan River at the edge of **Monument Valley** that is home to less than 100 people. You

will not be going that far. In fact, **this is far south as you will be venturing on your trip**. ***https://en.wikipedia.org/wiki/Mexican_Hat,_Utah***

- Drive to the **San Juan Inn** and check into your motel and then have a tasty dinner.
- Go **stargazing** from the banks of the **San Juan River**.

Insider Tips

- At the Twin Rocks Cafe, you can recharge your electronics from the electric plugs at each table and catch up on the latest and the greatest with their **FREE!** Wi-Fi.
- While you are in Monticello, Blanding, and Bluff, take a few minutes to drive around some of the side streets and check out the houses. Even though Bluff is by far the smallest of the three, there are some very interesting brick and wood frame houses. It's always fun to see how the locals live. The Mormons, as a rule, are very tidy folk who keep their properties looking nice with flowers and well-tended yards.

Save Money!

- The Monticello Visitor Center and Museum is **FREE!**
- Before you leave the Monticello Visitor Center, Edge of the Cedars Museum, and the San Juan Co-Operative Visitor Center, pick up the **FREE! park maps**, especially for the areas where you will be traveling next.
- Fort Bluff is **FREE!**
- The Bluff Cemetery is **FREE!**
- The Chacoan Great House is **FREE!**
- Sand Island is **FREE!**
- Mexican Hat is **FREE!**

Day Ten

NATURAL BRIDGES NATIONAL MONUMENT

This is going to be a wild day and you are going to cover a lot of ground. You will end up driving about 160 miles!

Over the course of the day, you will see the meandering Goosenecks of the San Juan River; the Valley of the Gods; and drive the Moki Dugway, a dirt and stone route that was featured on the show "Death Defying Roads", cut straight out of a canyon wall.

You will stand at a jaw-dropping overlook in the clouds where you can see four states.

You will then travel through a realm of glorious redrock and cedar trees that has the distinction of having the highest concentration of Indian ruins in the entire Southwest, before stopping at an amazing National Park crowned with spectacular natural bridges where you will do a fun hike framed by the controversial Bears Ears.

You will end your day cruising by several surreal sandstone monoliths on your way past the ghost village of Hite that has been marooned by the receding waters of Lake Powell.

And finally, you will land at a crossroads town in the absolute middle of nowhere. So, buckle up and let's get cracking!

How to Get There

After checking out of your hotel, head over to Gooseneck State Park:

- Drive back the way you came on US 163 (4 miles)

- Turn left on UT 261 South. (1 mile)
- Turn left on UT 316. (3.5 miles)

After visiting Gooseneck State Park retrace your route back to UT 261:

- Turn Left on UT 261 and head north. (8.8 miles)
- When you get to the top of the switchbacks, look for a left hand turn onto **Muley Point Road** about 0.2 of a mile after the top (just before the pavement begins). This is a wide, well-maintained sandy gravel road appropriate for all vehicles. It ends at **one of the most spectacular vistas in the Southwest**, (3.8 miles)

After checking out the view from the Muley Point Overlook:

- Backtrack on the gravel road and then turn left onto UT 261 North. (23 miles)
- Turn left on UT 95. (1.8 miles)
- Turn right onto UT 275 North to Natural Bridges National Monument. (3.8 miles)

After visiting Natural Bridges, backtrack to UT 95 and turn right to Hanksville, Utah. (91 miles)

Where to Stay

- **Whispering Sands** Motel in Hanksville, Utah
  http://www.whisperingsandsmotel.com/

Camping

- **Duke's Skickrock Grill, Campground & RV Park** in Hanksville, Utah
  https://www.dukesslickrock.com/
- The nearest **FREE!** Primitive camping on BLM land can be found a few miles **north** of Hanksville. Follow US 24 north until you are out of town and then take one of the wide gravel roads heading

off to the right until you find a place where you would like to camp.

Where to Eat

- Breakfast - **San Juan Inn & Trading Post** ***http://www.sanjuaninn.net/***
- Lunch - Snacks
- Dinner - **Duke's SlickRock Grill** in Hanksville, Utah. They serve some excellent IPA's and wine. Their pies are homemade. They brand their hamburger buns like cattle. And you can get your picture snapped at the bar, standing next to a life-size John "Duke" Wayne, in full cowboy regalia.

Best Things to Do

- You will need to get an early start, so eat breakfast and check out of your hotel **no later than 9AM**. **Make sure you download Natural Bridges on your Google maps for future reference when you are offline**. From here until Hanksville there will be no **Wi-Fi, services**, and the **only water will be at Natural Bridges**. But you will be more than compensated because this part of America provides nothing but spectacular views and blazing redrocks.
- Drive to **Goosenecks State Park**. The entrance road winds through high desert and ends at a spectacular overlook above the **Goosenecks**. As you stand there on the awe-inspiring rim and stare down into the deep gorge you will witness the raw power of nature. The ancient **San Juan River** in its more muscular days carved a series of winding bends through the soft sandstone that now rise into the sky like curvy buttes of brown delight, resembling colossal Goosenecks. It's like a painting of an imaginary place, especially in the shady morning light. ***https://stateparks.utah.gov/parks/goosenecks/***
- Drive up the **Moki Dugway**. **UT 261** climbs north from the San Juan River through the **Valley of the Gods** until it comes to a thousand-foot-tall battleship wall of imposing red sandstone.

Most sensible people would just turn around and go back. But not the Mormons. Where sane people saw an impediment, the Mormons saw opportunity. So, they dynamited a series of long straight switchbacks across the sheer rock face of the imposing plateau, hauled in some gravel, threw up some road signs, and called it the **Moki Dugway** (Moki is a silly made-up white man's word for "Hopi"). It's about five miles of white knuckle driving up into the clouds with scary cliff drops on the outside edge where there is no guardrail. To make it even more interesting, blocks of Kayenta sandstone often drop from the mesa walls and litter the roadway like land mines, adding just a little more terror to your drive as you dodge the rocks by getting perilously close to the edge. Perhaps this is why UT 261 was featured on the TV show **"Death Defying Roads"**.
http://bluffutah.org/mokey-dugway-muley-point/

- Drive to the Muley Point Overlook. When you get to the top of the Moki Dugway, turn left onto a wide gravel road. This road goes for about four miles and is sandy. In several low spots you will feel your vehicle begin to slowly slide sideways. But if you just maintain your speed at about 30 mph, so you don't get stuck, and don't overreact, you will do just fine. At the end of the road you will come to Muley Point, one of the most incredible viewpoints on earth. No matter how many times I see it, it is still a wonder to behold the unbelievable views from this majestic mesa top in the clouds. Standing on the perilous edge of a thousand-foot escarpment that looks like it has been cut by god like a piece of wedding cake, you can see four states: Navajo Mountain to your right is in Arizona), Shiprock is straight ahead in New Mexico, to your left are the snowy San Juan Mountains in Colorado, and you are standing in Utah overlooking the Valley of the Gods. Amazing!
https://utah.com/monument-valley/valley-of-the-gods
- Drive across **Cedar Mesa**. This land of pinyon-juniper and spacey slickrock canyons has the **highest concentration of Anasazi ruins in the entire Southwest**. The Anasazi were everywhere around this primeval area from before the time

of Christ until about 1300 AD. Why here? Because it provided everything they needed and desired within easy walking distance and was easy on the eyes. There were spacious sandstone overhangs to keep them sheltered from the weather; abundant springs and seeps; arable bottom land right below their high and dry homes; plentiful wood for fire; edible and medicinal plants in abundance; large and small game all around; and a wide variety of materials from which they could make clothing, tools, and weapons. It was not too hot and not too cold. It was just right.
https://utah.com/monument-valley/cedar-mesa

- Drive through Cedar Mesa's **Grand Gulch Primitive Area**. You will pass the **Cane Gulch Ranger Station** on your right. You need a permit to hike into this twisting maze of slot canyons, much of which is a designated wilderness area closed to all things with a motor, and the Park Service takes their protection job very seriously. The rangers can provide you with the latest weather and road conditions. This is a place where you need to be very careful. It is very easy to get lost. And the roads are sand traps. In short, **don't go into Grand Gulch unless you are an experienced canyoneer**, and even then, things can get tricky really, really fast.
- You will catch some great views of the **Bears Ears** as you approach Natural Bridges. The Bears Ears are the two black buttes that look sort of like giant bears ears, perched above **Natural Bridges National Monument**. They are sacred to the **Navajo, Ute, and Puebloan Indians**. According to Navajo legend, the voluptuous **Changing-Bear Maiden** was fooled by the trickster **Coyote** into marriage. Soon she started turning into a bear. The maiden's two older brothers decided to quickly change her into something else before it was too late. So, they killed her. Then they chopped off her ears and threw them away. And that's where the Bears Ears buttes came from. As with many Navajo tales, the lesson is unclear. Killing your sister doesn't really transform her into anything but dead. It's just another story of men abusing unruly women, if you ask me.

- But the real controversy surrounding Bears Ears is its National Monument status. President Obama made it **America's newest National Monument** right before he left office and that seriously angered many of the locals who felt that there was already too much protected federal land, of which the Bears Ears was a longstanding part, and **WAY too many Monuments**, which come with even more restrictions prohibiting things like mining and firewood cutting. So, Trump's new Interior Secretary recommended **reducing the Monument's size**, while **maintaining the Monument status for the area surrounding the Bears Ears**. And then all hell broke loose. The locals rejoiced, and the enviros went crazy.
- After living in the Southwest for many years, I am ambivalent about the issue. To further protect the Bears Ears, which was already protected, President Obama created a **Monument** that stretched for hundreds of miles, encompassing thousands of acres of land - from **Dead Horse State Park** above Moab in the north, to **Goosenecks State Park** in the South. The rationale was to create a consistent management area encompassing a huge and diverse swath of federal lands that could be protected as **one cohesive National Monument *ecosystem.*** And that's all well and good. But in a hardscrabble place inhabited by stubborn and often belligerent Mormons just trying to scratch a living from an unforgiving landscape, it smacked of arrogant overreach. The land in question is not a vacation spot for these hardworking people, it is their **home**. And while they love the Bears Ears as much as the next person and **do not oppose its designation as a National Monument**, they see no reason why the government should essentially lock down a huge part of Utah to appease a bunch of people who have no idea where the Bears Ears National Monument is even located. And to be honest, I think they're right. In the end, the expansion of the Monument under Obama was a clever way to stop the extractive industries from laying waste to the fragile landscape, and really had little or nothing to do with protecting Bears Ears. And that's a noble cause. But to expand the acreage or reduce it

was really just a business squeeze play with the poor Mormons who live there caught in the middle. ***http://www.standard.net/Environment/2016/12/29/why-is-bears-ears-national-monument-controversy-obama-big-deal***

- Drive to **Natural Bridges National Monument -** Given its remote location, **Natural Bridges** is one of the most lightly visited parks in America. And that's a shame because it is a real gem. The **Visitor Center** is outstanding, and their gift shop is filled with interesting items and exhibits. The park is very user friendly. Essentially, it features three large natural bridges that were made millions of years ago when long dried up creeks blasted them open – **versus arches which are created by intrusions of water from above**. And just for your viewing pleasure they throw in a few Anasazi ruins. You can just drive the **9-mile, one-way loop road** and stop at the overlooks, or you can take the short, but steep, trails to the bottom of **White Canyon** and stand under the spectacular behemoths.
- Interestingly, Sipapu Bridge has always been listed as the **fourth largest natural Bridge in the world**, measuring a gargantuan **240 feet**, but the National Park Service recently got around to accurately measuring it with a laser and discovered that it was actually only **143 feet**. Quite the error, even by Parkie standards. No matter, your two or three hours visit to Natural Bridges will make your eyes flutter and your heart sing. ***https://www.nps.gov/nabr/index.htm***
- Drive through Fry Canyon. Sandy Johnson, a local lady, used to operate a sort of hippie/cowboy lodge in Fry Canyon about twenty miles from Natural Bridges when I was roaming around Canyon Country back in the Eighties. I always stopped there for a tasty meal and some good conversation whenever I was passing through. She had a few rundown motel rooms and a cafe where she served good eats and sold drinks (beer) and snacks. The sagebrush flat in front of the place was adorned with weird sculptures made from castoff construction materials like pipe and machinery. There was a pool table and there were usually a few locals hanging out. It was the only place where you could

get a home cooked meal between the San Juan Trading Post and Hanksville. In its heyday it was one of the uranium capitals of the United States. There was a temporary town there with over 3,000 miners, many of whom ultimately died from radiation exposure, and they served more beer in Fry Canyon than in Salt Lake City. It's a broiling hot and windswept place. There was no electricity and water needed to be hauled in. In winter, it was a frigid ghost town. On my most recent visit in 2017, we had camped the night before at Muley Point and hadn't eaten a cooked meal since the Twin Rocks Cafe in Bluff the day before. And after hiking in Natural Bridges we were starved. But as we approached the old oasis, it was obvious the place wasn't open. The sculptures were gone, and the front door was open, swaying in the wind like a time port into the Twilight Zone.
https://en.wikipedia.org/wiki/Fry_Canyon,_Utah

- Drive through **White Canyon** - As you drive along the **Bicentennial Highway** – the road that was vandalized at the end of Edward Abbey's classic tale "The Monkey Wrench Gang" – heading west from Natural Bridges, White Canyon, the creek that created Natural Bridges is on your right all the way to Hite, a once booming boat launch/convenience store run by the National Park Service concessionaire at the head of Lake Powell. There are numerous slot canyon hikes – some quite dangerous. And there are several very wild geologic monoliths, like the **Cheesebox** and **Jacob's Chair**, dotting the surreal landscape to your right. Take the time to stop and just take in the beauty of this remote area of America. And snap a photo at the *Jetsons Bridge* over the Colorado River. Look for the airplane landing strip on the left after the bridge. When Hite was rocking back in the eighties, there were small planes landing and taking off regularly.
https://www.nps.gov/glca/planyourvisit/hite.htm
- Drive past **The Rocks Swimming Hole** - There's a spot near the confluence of the Colorado River and the Dirty Devil River where a giant wedge of Navajo Sandstone squeezes UT 95 and creates a doorway effect. Over the years, at least three different

car commercials have been filmed there. In 1981, on my first foray into this lonely part of the Colorado Plateau, I discovered a path by this spot that led down to the lake. There were a series of small islands stretching out into the lake, and I would wade and swim my way out to the end of the chain where there were shady alcoves and diving rocks. The lake was deep. I called my secret swimming hole the "diving rocks spa". When we drove by on our way to Hanksville in 2017, my treasured swimming spot had been transformed into a lake-bleached, white knobby mountain of rock with grass and bushes growing in front of it. The prolonged drought is slowly changing the face of the Southwest and even the monster dams cannot stop the baking process.

- Stop at the **Hite Overlook** - UT 95 climbs out of the Lake Powell basin and there's an amazing overlook with a stupendous (and sad) view of a dried-up lake. Entire campgrounds where people used to swim and tie their boats are now a hundred feet up in the air and a mile from the lake. The headwaters of the lake are stagnant brown from the **Dirty Devil River** which was named by the **Powell Expedition** and is now but a trickle. And the Colorado River is a mere shadow of its finer self. Hite still is in operation, but the Park Service had to build a new concrete ramp a couple hundred yards long, so people can get their boats to the lake. There is a small convenience store/gas station during the boating season. Most people now access the upper end of Lake Foul at **Hall's Crossing** or **Bullfrog**, and Hite has the lonely feel of being the last outpost. After almost twenty years of drought in the Southwest, the brimming turquoise lakes and the azure blue skies are but a fleeting memory. ***http://www.amwest-travel.com/utah-lake-powell-hite.html***
- Stop and check into your motel in **Hanksville**. The little oasis of Hanksville sits just to the north of the **Henry Mountains.** The Henry's were the **last mountain range in the lower forty-eight** to be discovered and the nearby town of **Boulder** was the **last city to get mail delivery**. It's pretty much the back of

beyond and about as far away from anything that you can get in America south of Alaska.
https://utah.com/henry-mountains

- There isn't a lot to see and do in Hanksville. The highway running through town serves as Main Street. There's a funky **Visitor Center/Medical Clinic** combo by the intersection with **UT 24**, across from the **Hollow Mountain gas station** which is a must stop roadside attraction. There's a small grocery store on the west end of town and a post office. There are two motels. There's **Blondies** for breakfast, **Stan's Burger Shack** for lunch, and **Duke's** for dinner. Dukes also has a nice campground and rustic cabins. There is a **year-round car repair** shop about a mile out of town on UT 24. And that's pretty much it. It's a hot dusty place to bed down on the way to **Capitol Reef.** I often called it the heart of nowhere. But in its own weird way, it seems dreamy, like a science fiction movie with a happy ending.
https://en.wikipedia.org/wiki/Hanksville,_Utah
- After dinner, go **stargazing** from right in front of your hotel room. Just set up your lawn chair in the giant parking lot of the Whispering Sands and take in the sky show. There aren't a lot of lights in Hanksville so the stars are easy to spot, and you don't have to get in your car and drive out of town to see them.

Best Hikes

- You can do the individual trails at **Natural Bridges National Monument** one at a time (see below), or you can just do the Loop Trail and see tall three of the main bridges all in one continuous circuit. This is the trail I always take, but you might not want to hike so far, or might not have enough time and would prefer to do them individually.
- **Loop Trail** - The 8.6-mile (13.8 km) loop trail provides an excellent way to experience the wonders of all the Natural Bridges. The full loop passes all three bridges, but you can also take shorter loops between the bridges. Join the loop trail at any of the bridge parking areas. If you want to hike the full loop, follow

the trail up the left side of the canyon after passing Kachina Bridge to skirt the "Knickpoint" pour-off.

- **Sipapu Bridge** - This is one of the largest natural bridges in the United States (Rainbow Bridge on Lake Powell is the biggest). In Hopi mythology, a "Sipapu" is a gateway through which souls may pass to the spirit world. The trail to the canyon bottom below Sipapu is the steepest in the park. A staircase and **three wooden ladders** aid in the descent. At the top of the stairway, notice the logs reaching out from the cliff wall to the large fir tree on the other side of the stairs. Early visitors to the park climbed down this tree to reach the canyon. At the base of the tree you can still see the remains of an earlier staircase. The ledge located halfway down the trail provides an excellent view of Sipapu Bridge. Please use caution around the cliff edges. The remaining portion of the trail leads down a series of switchbacks and ladders to the grove of Gambel's oak beneath Sipapu. (1.2 miles - 1 hour)
  Elevation change: 500 feet
- **Kachina Bridge** - This is a massive bridge and is considered the "youngest" of the three because of the thickness of its span. The relatively small size of its opening and its orientation make it difficult to see from the overlook. The pile of boulders under the far side of the bridge resulted from a rockfall in 1992, when approximately 4,000 tons of rock broke off the bridge. As you descend the switchbacks, notice the "Knickpoint" pour-off in Armstrong Canyon below and to your left. During floods, this spout sends a muddy red waterfall plunging into the pool below. The bridge is named for the Kachina dancers that play a central role in Hopi religious tradition. There is a bathroom at the trailhead. (1.4 miles - 1 hour)
  Elevation change: 400 feet
- **Owachomo Bridge** - The word means "rock mound" in Hopi and is named after the rock formation on top of the southeast end of the bridge. From the overlook, the twin buttes called "The Bear's Ears" (America's newest National Monument) break the eastern horizon. The original road to Natural Bridges

passed between these buttes, ending across the canyon from Owachomo Bridge at the original visitor center (which was a platform tent). The old trail still winds up the other side of the canyon but is seldom used. Notice that Tuwa Creek no longer flows under Owachomo like it did for thousands of years. The bridge's delicate form suggests that it is has eroded more quickly than the other bridges. This is the shortest and easiest of the three hikes. (0.4 miles - 30 minutes)
Elevation change: 108 feet

- **Horsecollar Ruin** - There is a short and fairly flat trail across the slickrock to an impressive overlook above the Horsecollar Ruin in the bottom of White Canyon. This is a good place to better appreciate how the Anasazi lived back in the day. (0.6 roundtrip)

Insider Tips

- Once you leave the San Juan Trading Post you will not be able to get a reliable internet connection or probably even cell phone service until you end the day in Hanksville. Be sure to download Natural Bridges from Google maps before you leave the San Juan Trading post, so you have a GPS map!
- The only drinking between the San Juan Trading Post and Hanksville will be at Natural Bridges. You might get lucky with the store at Hite, but that can be hot or miss and involves a fairly long detour to the lake.
- A few miles west of Natural Bridges at the junction of **UT 95, the Bicentennial Highway**, and the turnoff to **Hall's Crossing (Lake Powell)** is a popular spot used by the local police for **DUI checkpoints**. If you have an open liquor container, and that would **include an opened bottle of liquor or wine in your trunk**, you are going to get hit with a $75 fine. They don't take checks or credit cards. And if you can't pay, they will haul your ass to jail in Monticello. I learned this lesson the hard way back in 1992, when I came upon the road block after almost dying in the **Black Box in White Canyon**, following a killer hike.

- While the air is still clearer than any east coast sky, you can't help but notice the smoke. After almost twenty years of drought with below average rainfall in the West, our forests, parks, and brushlands have been turned into fire traps. And every summer the fire season starts earlier and lasts a bit longer. As a result, the skies that used to be so crystal blue and almost shiny, are now perpetually filtered by a smoky haze. And you don't have to be near a fire for it to affect the clarity of the sky. The prevailing winds can blow smoke into the Southwest from as far away as the Pacific Northwest or the Inter-Mountain West, meaning a fire in a national forest in Idaho can bring a smoky haze to the Four Corners Region. And while it might not smell like smoke, it still fouls the air. Welcome to the new normal.
- There is a clean bathroom at the **Hog Springs rest area** a few miles past the Hite Overlook. It's worth the stop to see the honeycombs in the sandstone walls.

Save Money!

- If you get to the Goosenecks State Park before nine, there is a good chance that there will be no one at the gate to charge you an admission fee, which means you will get into the park for **FREE!**
- The Muley Point Overlook is **FREE!**
- Before you leave the San Juan Trading Post and the Natural Bridges National Monument Visitor Center and the, pick up the **FREE! park maps**, especially for the areas where you will be traveling next.

Day Eleven

LITTLE WILD HORSE SLOT CANYON

Today you are going to explore one of the finest and most accessible slot canyons in the Southwest, and because it's located in the back of beyond it doesn't get thousands of people visiting it each day like so many of the national parks in the region. Plus, you must get out of your car and hike to see it. So, that keeps the numbers down. But it is still quite popular with the people of Utah, so you should expect to see a fair number of people.

After your hike through Goblin Valley you will drive through an enchanting world of extremes, filled with lushly irrigated valleys, multi-colored mesas, the Caineville Buttes, the Bentonite Badlands. Goblin Valley.

And you will end your day at one of my favorite National Parks, Capitol Reef National Park.

This will definitely be a day for the ol' memory bank.

How to Get There

- Turn onto UT 24 East by the red & white Sandstone Dome gas station in Hanksville. (19.6 miles)
- Turn left onto Temple Mt. Road. (5.2 miles)
- Turn left onto Goblin Valley Road. (6.7 miles)
- As you approach the entrance station to the state park, turn right to the trailhead. (5.3 miles)

After hiking Little Wild Horse Canyon slot canyon:

- Backtrack to UT 24 West and return to Hanksville. (36.8 miles)

- Turn right onto UT 24 West and drive to Capitol Reef National Park and Torrey, Utah. (48 miles)

Where to Stay

- **Capitol Reef Resort** in Torrey, Utah. This place has it all! A great restaurant, horseback rides, and is centrally located for everything you want to see and do. It also has reliable Wi-Fi, something that many of the hotels around Torrey do not. **They say they do**, and it's usually free, but it tends to be spotty. ***https://capitolreefresort.com/***

Camping

- **Capitol Reef National Park Campground**. This is a lovely campground with trails along the river and to the historic town of Fruita. This is one of the best National Park campgrounds in the U.S.
  https://www.nps.gov/care/planyourvisit/campinga.htm
- **Wonderland RV Park** in Torrey
  http://www.capitolreefrvpark.com/
- **Most of the land around Torrey is either private or national park land. So, I would strongly recommend that you camp in one of the commercial campgrounds in Torrey.**

Where to Eat

- Breakfast - **Blondie's Eatery & Gift** in Hanksville
  https://www.tripadvisor.com/Restaurant_Review-g57006-d729545-Reviews-Blondie_s_Eatery_Gift-Hanksville_Utah.html
- Lunch - **Luna Mesa is** 19 miles east of Hanksville on the way to Capitol Reef. Simple, yet tasty Mexican fare.
  https://www.tripadvisor.com/Restaurant_Review-g60758-d3738817-Reviews-Luna_Mesa_Oasis-Torrey_Utah.html
- **Stan's Burger Shack** in Hanksville, Utah
  http://www.stansburgershak.com/

- Dinner - **Broken Spur Steak House** in Torrey, Utah. This place is a bit hard to find but it's a local favorite. As you crest the hill on UT24 coming into the town of Torrey, look for a sign for the restaurant and a road leading up onto a hill. There are fancier restaurants in Torrey, but after a long day of hiking and driving, you are probably just going to want to check into your hotel and grab a quick bite to eat. And more importantly, it has great views from atop the hill overlooking Capitol Reef, is close to the park. That means you will have a shorter drive back into the park after dinner for the ranger talk.
  https://brokenspurinn.com/the-steakhouse/
- **La Cueva** serves large helpings of authentic Mexican food and is near your hotel. This is even closer to the park and right off the highway on the right.
  http://www.cafelacueva.com/

Best Things to Do

- You should eat breakfast and check out of your hotel by **9AM**.
- Before heading over to Goblin Valley, you need to stop at **Hollow Mountain** for some gas, snacks, and water. The store was carved out of the inside of a brown sandstone hill and it is like walking into a big cave. They sell a little bit of everything, including an excellent assortment of Michael Kelsey guide books, which I was amazed to discover are now in their fifth printing. His original book "Canyon Hiking Guide to the COLORADO PLATEAU" was my hiking bible for many years. My, how time flies when you're having fun.
  https://www.roadsideamerica.com/tip/1314
- Hike **Little Wild Horse Slot Canyon** in Goblin Valley. **Goblin Valley** is in a **state park** and on **BLM land**. The state park is noted for its hoodoos and weird balanced-rock formations and is extremely popular with the people of Utah who come from far and wide to play amidst the odd assortment of rock formations.
- Goblin Valley was in the news in 2016, when some jerk decided to push one of the precariously perched rocks off its base.

And rather than own it, and just admit that he was an idiot, he claimed that he was performing a public service by knocking over the rock before it fell on some unsuspecting hiker. The authorities didn't buy his story and he went to jail and was subsequently convicted of being a jerk.
https://stateparks.utah.gov/parks/goblin-valley/

- Back in Hanksville after your hike, stop briefly at the **Visitor Center** to check on road conditions and any alerts.
- Drive west on UT 24 and experience one of my favorite Southwest drives through the **Fremont River Valley**, the **San Rafael Swell**, and the **Caineville Mesas**. It is a starkly beautiful land of brown-stained and red-streaked battleship mesas and irrigated farmlands.
https://en.wikipedia.org/wiki/Fremont_River_(Utah)
- Eat lunch at **Luna Mesa**. But check their website to make sure they are still in business. If they aren't, then eat lunch at **Stan's Burger Shack** in Hanksville.

  Luna Mesa is the only place to eat between Hanksville and Torrey. It's a hippie/cosmic outpost that serves home cooked Mexican food. Back in the eighties I often stopped there on my way through the area to grab a beer and take in the goofy interior that was papered in money from all around the world. But like the Fry Canyon Lodge, businesses have a short shelf life in this part of America given the small number of local inhabitants and the marginal tourist traffic passing through the area. Plus, the place looks a little weird, starting with the name, and that can reduce your business. So, it is always wise to check in advance to see if the place where you want to eat is still in operation. In 2017, Luna Mesa was still going strong, though under fresh management. A young couple, **Dan and Cher**, along with their new baby girl, will welcome you with open arms. They serve simple food, but it's delicious, food and clearly made with love. It's like dining in someone's funky kitchen and it's definitely a **"Best of the Southwest"** kind of stop.

- After passing the entrance sign to Capitol Reef National Park, you still have a way to go. Your first stop is a few miles inside the park at the historic **Behunin Cabin** which is listed on the National Register. The one room stone house measures 13' x 17' and **Elijah Behunin and his wife and thirteen children** lived there in 1883 for only one year before pulling up stakes and moving up-canyon to the nearby town of **Fruita**. Man, you talk about a tough life.
  https://en.wikipedia.org/wiki/Elijah_Cutler_Behunin_Cabin
- Hike the **Grand Wash Trail**. There is a sign for the trail along the highway. Pull into the roadside pullout along UT 24 by a small bridge over a dry wash of boulders in a grove of big cotton-wood trees. By hitting this trail toward the end of the day you will beat the heat and the crowds.
- Continue along UT 24, stopping at the long pull out to snap some photos of the **Capitol Dome**, a colossal white dome of Navajo Sandstone that closely resembles the **Capitol Building in Washington, D.C.**
- Head past all the attractions in the historic town of Fruita. You will check these sites out tomorrow. But stop at the Visitor Center very briefly to see about the evening ranger talk. If the Visitor Center is closed, look for a sign by the front door telling you when the talk will begin that evening. Wait until tomorrow to revisit the Visitor Center, see the movie, and check out the exhibits and gift shop.
  https://www.nps.gov/care/index.htm
- Proceed north toward the town of Torrey and check into your motel.
  http://www.torreyutah.com/
- Go to dinner and then head back to the park and catch the **evening ranger talk in the amphitheater by the campground and river**. The ranger talks usually begins right before dark and there is one every night.
  https://www.nps.gov/care/planyourvisit/ranger-programs.htm

Best Hikes

- **Little Wild Horse Canyon** - Some of the finest narrows in the Southwest and a flat and very easy hike. Because it is just five miles from the popular Goblin Valley State Park, this amazing canyon is easily explored and has narrow passages as fine as any other Southwest slot canyon. **Little Wild Horse Canyon** has become the most visited location in the **San Rafael Swell**. It will take at least three hours to see the best sections along its lower end, although the usual plan is to combine a tour with neighboring Bell Canyon - this is an 8-mile loop that in addition to the two narrow gorges also passes high, colorful cliffs and very interesting exposed and eroded rock. There are various places good for camping further along the access road - pleasant, free alternatives to the nearby paid site in the state park. ***http://www.americansouthwest.net/utah/san_rafael_swell/index.html***

  You do **not** want to go to **Goblin Valley State Park**. And it will cost you **$13** to get into the park. The place is usually overrun with Mormon school children and church groups, and it isn't worth the cost or the time. You have better things to see.

  As you are approaching the entrance station to the state park, look for a right hand turn onto a paved road. Take that road to the trailhead which is a large parking lot with a bathroom and some information signs. This parking lot fills up fast, so it is wise to get there early.

  The main narrows of Little Wild Horse Canyon can be reached after just ten minutes walking from the trailhead, though they are easily missed as the entrance is a concealed slit in the right side of the canyon.

  The first half-mile of the hike is along a wide open dry wash with the occasional cottonwood tree providing some much-needed shade. Please keep in mind that this is a very hot place and temperatures often reach **100 degrees**. Once you are in the narrows, the heat will no longer be a factor. But getting to the narrows and back can be a hot proposition.

When the canyon starts to tighten up you will need to avoid the first narrow section which is a dead end that turns into a slimy red mud bog ending in a slippery rock wall. Look for a well-worn trail to the left that leads up onto a sandstone ledge. Follow the ledge for a few hundred feet until the trail drops back down into the narrow canyon beyond the mud trap.

You are now at the intersection of **Bell Canyon** and **Little Wild Horse Canyon**. There is a very hard-to-see directional sign post on the sand bench in front of you, indicating that **you should take the canyon on the right**. **Bell is the larger, main canyon to the left**.

Once you enter Little Wild Horse Canyon the narrows begin almost immediately and run pretty much continuously for the next two miles. It is slow going but there is nothing too difficult or challenging. Just take your time and stop frequently to enjoy the amazing spectacle of one of the Southwest's premier **slot canyons**.

The first time I had hiked the isolated canyon, back in the early eighties, I had the place completely to myself. Little Wild Horse had yet to be discovered. But now it's on everyone's bucket list, so there will be lots of hikers – mostly smiling Mormon families with small children. And given how narrow the trail is, you will often have to stop periodically to let people coming back down the canyon pass by because there isn't enough room for more than one person at a time.

Little Wild Horse is so narrow that in some places the walls of the canyon come together and there is no ground to stand on. So, you must walk sideways on the canyon walls. The smooth rock faces are polished and fluted like magnificent sculptures that would put any man-made piece of art to shame. The scale is immense and the colors psychedelic.

- At the two miles mark the canyon opens up for a quarter mile and then comes to a large stagnant pool. This is as far as you will be going. You can hike up the canyon a few more miles to where it intersects with Bell Canyon, and then turn left and hike back to where you started. But once the narrows end, the rest of the trail is wide open and often dangerously hot. So, stop at the end of the narrow section, eat a snack and drink some water, and relax before heading back down canyon to the trailhead. Take your time and enjoy your second trip through the narrows because you are never going to see anything like them again in your life. And the hike back is never as fun as going up because there is no sense of exploration. But novelty is a relative term in a place like Little Wild Horse. It is an absolutely magical place. (4 miles - 3 hrs)

http://www.americansouthwest.net/slot_canyons/little_wild_horse_canyon/

- This **Grand Wash Trail** - This is an up and back hike like Little Wild Horse, in a narrow and deep canyon, but that is where the similarities end. Hike up the deep narrow canyon a little over two miles, to the trailhead at the head of the canyon off the **Scenic Drive**, and then turn around and walk back to your car, a 4.5-mile amble through a world of eroding **Jurassic** rock encompassing **200 million years** of watery upheaval. **Grand Wash** is one of the most popular trails in Capitol Reef, so you should expect to see other hikers, especially in the upper end. The canyon follows the meander bends of the powerful river that originally carved the canyon and as the sun moves across the sky, you will find lots of shade along one side of the canyon or the other. When the sun hits the black iron streaks of **desert varnish** on the white **Navajo Sandstone** walls they look like the surreal images in a **Juan Miro** painting. In some places the **Kayenta Sandstone** walls are honeycombed with weird **water-pockets** that look like big ice cream scoops have been spooned out of the red rock. It is like geology gone mad. Keep your eyes peeled for **desert bighorn sheep** that often stand defiantly on the precarious ledges like silent sentinels. As you get closer to the trailhead at the head of the canyon you will undoubtedly start seeing and hearing more hikers. The hike back down-canyon is always a bit anticlimactic. But all in all, your three-hour cruise through Grand Wash was a pure delight.

https://utah.com/hiking/capitol-reef-national-park/grand-wash

Insider Tips

- If you continue past the trailhead for Little Wild Horse, it will eventually take you all the way to I-70. But the road is unpaved, and the surface deteriorates somewhat as it follows a stony streambed; the road eventually meets Muddy Creek, the main river in the southern Swell, just downstream of its lengthy narrows section ('**The Chute**'). There are many good camp sites.
- You are probably wondering: **What's the difference between a slot canyon and a narrows?** Well, as I learned during the evening ranger talk entitled "Slot Canyons" in the lovely moonlit Amphitheater at **Capitol Reef National Park**, the terms are not interchangeable. **Ranger Adam** explained to us how he had tried to research the topic and "hit a wall" because there really was no standard definition for the term. So, Adam started asking his canyoneer friends for their definition and they collectively narrowed it down to this: **a slot canyon is where you can touch both canyon walls with your arms**. Narrows can only be called slot canyons if they are **really** narrow. I came up with another defining factor for slot canyons: **if you are in a slot canyon when a flash flood comes barreling through, you're toast**; whereas in a narrows, you might be able to find some high ground. As an example, Little Wild Horse is a slot canyon, and Capitol Wash is a narrows; it's pretty narrow, but it's still too wide to be called a slot canyon. The **Wingate** and **Navajo Sandstone** geologic formations are where you will find a slot canyon. Nobody has any idea how many slot canyons there are in the Colorado Plateau, but there are more than in any place else on earth.
- Wi-Fi at a lot of places in the Torrey and the Capitol Reef area is spotty. The **Capitol Reef Resort** has reliable internet and it's **FREE!**

- The **Capitol Reef Resort** has an outstanding and cheap breakfast buffet every morning, with fresh fruit that will save you money, offering a wide selection of food.

Save Money!

- The ranger talk at Capitol Reef is **FREE!**
- Before you leave the Hanksville Visitor Center, pick up the **FREE! park maps**, especially for the areas where you will be traveling next.

Day Twelve

CAPITOL REEF NATIONAL PARK

I used to say that Capitol Reef was the hidden gem of National Parks that no one knew about. Well, the world has finally found it. The Visitor Center is like a bus station and the tour buses roll in like clockwork. The most popular trails are often packed, and while it isn't as jammed as Arches National Park, it often seems quite crowded, mainly because so many of the attractions are bunched together around Fruita and the Visitor Center. The parking lots are usually full, the trails can often resemble a parade route, and the narrow, winding roads are busy. So, even though you are far removed from civilization, you need to be prepared to deal with lots of happy travelers.

I don't want to come across like I'm demeaning these other park visitors. Everyone has a right to experience nature, and I would rather they hike the canyons of the Southwest than sit on their couches watching football or Oprah. We all have the same rights when it comes to visiting our national parks. They are for everybody to enjoy in their own way if they follow the rules and treat these treasures and their fellow travelers with respect. But, it is just more enjoyable when you are the only one there. You feel like it's all yours.

That said, your last big day in the wild is going to be a truly wonderful experience, full of hiking, history, geology, and great food.

You will begin your morning with a delicious breakfast buffet before hitting the trail for an enchanting hike along the Fremont River.

Then it's off to the historic town of Fruita where you will pick fruit in their beautiful orchards.

After that, you will visit a thousand-year-old Indian rock art panel and then learn about the rugged pioneers who settled in this watery paradise surrounded by imposing canyons.

And then you will stop by a historic farm house where they serve some of the tastiest fruit pies you have ever sampled. Who doesn't like pie?

You will then hop in your car and take the mesmerizing and extremely informative Scenic Drive into the Capitol Gorge, ending with a hike into a narrow, redrock canyon that will take your breath away.

And you will end your day lounging on the back patio of a rustic inn overlooking Capitol Reef as the sun goes down, eating tasty local delicacies.

Capitol Reef is a world of opposites working in harmony. It's technically a desert. It only gets about ten inches of rain a year. And most of the rain it does get comes in flash flood bursts. But it also has two rivers running through its heart, making it a land of extremes and overwhelming beauty.

Your next to last day in Canyonlands will be one that you will long remember!

How to Get There

- Drive Highway 24 East back into the park and go to the Visitor Center. (10 miles)

Where to Eat

- Breakfast - **Pioneer Kitchen at the Capitol Reef Resort**. They have a delectable breakfast buffet with a wide assortment of fruit and other tasty items for a very reasonable price. ***https://www.tripadvisor.com/ShowUserReviews-g60758-d9885237-r349461710-The_Pioneer_Kitchen-Torrey_Utah.html***

- Lunch - **Gifford House**. They have the best homemade fruit pies you ever tasted, plus other hot-out-of-the-oven bakery items. ***https://www.tripadvisor.com/Attraction_Review-g143017-d1503679-Reviews-Gifford_Homestead-Capitol_Reef_National_Park_Utah.html***
- Dinner - **Rim Rock Inn** in Torrey, Utah. Scrumptious local food with sweeping sunset views of Capitol Reef. ***http://www.therimrock.net/***

Best Things to Do

- Eat breakfast and start heading for the trailhead by **9AM**.
- Drive back to Capitol Reef and stop at **Panorama Point** on the right for some splendid views.
- Drive to the **Capitol Reef National Park Visitor Center**. The Visitor Center is quite busy and a bit cramped, but well worth the stop. Check out the bookstore which is stocked with some great natural history books and maps. And the movie "Watermarks" about the park is a must see. ***https://www.nps.gov/care/planyourvisit/hours.htm***
- Before you leave the Visitor Center, purchase the brochure entitled **"The Scenic Drive of Capitol Reef National Park – Self-Guided Driving Tour"** for **$2**.
- Hike the **Fremont River Trail**. ***https://liveandlethike.com/2015/02/26/fremont-river-trail-capitol-reef-national-park-ut/***
- Check out some of the roadside attractions around the **Fruita Rural History District**, starting with the **Jackson U-Pick orchard** where you will find yourself competing with the **wild turkeys and deer** for some ripe **apples, peaches and pears** that hang from the trees like tasty jewels and litter the ground like sour mash. After picking a small basket of fruit, return to the front gate, weigh your fruit on a little scale and pay your $5. It is strictly an honor system operation. ***https://www.nps.gov/care/learn/historyculture/orchard-scms.htm***

- Fruita was settled by the legendary Mormon homesteader **Nels Johnson** who was part of the **San Juan Mission** team that had been sent to **Bluff** on the **San Juan River** that you visited a few days before. Nels arrived in 1880 and built his one room cabin in what is now the **Chestnut Picnic Area**, near the largest cottonwood tree I have ever seen. It's called the **Mail Tree** because the mailman would put the mail in little wooden boxes that were attached to the gnarly old tree. Nels realized that his homestead, located at the confluence of the **Fremont River** and **Sulfur Creek**, was the perfect spot to grow **fruit and nut trees.** And as more settlers moved into the area, the valley bottom began blooming with orchards, many of which have survived to the present. According to the Parkies, it is one of the largest orchards in the National Park system with over **3,000 trees**!
- Continue east on Highway 24 and stop at the **petroglyph panel** where Indians have been chiseling their dreams since 600 AD. The huge parking lot is usually mobbed with buses and cars. The panel is rather disappointing (but worth about 15 minutes of your time) because the Park Service has built a new board-walk to limit direct access to the panel. In fact, they now keep visitors so far away that you can barely make out the drawings. They even have one of those goofy round metal binoculars like they put on the tops of tall buildings, so you can view the rock art from afar. If you have binoculars, bring them along. In the old days, the Parkies let you walk right up to the panel and see the glyphs up close, but given the increased visitation and threat of vandalism, they have decided to keep everyone at a safe distance.
  https://www.nps.gov/care/learn/historyculture/fremont.htm
- Head back toward the Visitor Center and make one last stop at the **Historic Fruita School**, a log cabin that is a bit strange because they have a small audio box by the window that is continuously broadcasting the voice of the school teacher instructing her students. Peer through the small window at the bare, one room school and try to imagine the Mormon children

sitting obediently at their desks, learning the alphabet and practicing addition.
https://www.nps.gov/care/learn/historyculture/fruitaschool-house.htm

- At this point, you can drive the fifteen miles into the town of **Torrey** to get some lunch. But that is going to burn up a lot of time. And time is precious. I suggest that you turn left at the Visitor Center and begin the Scenic Drive. After passing the Mail Tree and the Picnic Area, look for an old farmhouse on the right. This is the historic **Gifford House**, and they sell freshly-baked pies, using fruit from the local orchards. Who doesn't like pie? The historic **Gifford House** features a small **frontier museum and store**. And they have an incredible selection of large and small **fruit pies** and **fresh bread**. I love their mixed fruit pie. After you have purchased your pie and a cold drink, walk outside and eat your mouthwatering pie at a picnic table in the shade of a spreading cottonwood tree in the front yard.
https://www.nps.gov/care/learn/historyculture/gifford-homestead.htm
- After devouring your delightful pie, take the **10-mile Scenic Drive to Capitol Gorge**. You are starting at the hottest part of the day, so take it easy. Stop at all of the interpretive signs along the way where you will learn about: the rock formations; the creation of the **Waterpocket Fold**; the old **Oyler Mine** where uranium was mined from the yellowish-gray **Chinle Formation**; **Cassidy Arch** which was named after the outlaw **Butch Cassidy**, who supposedly used Capitol Reef for a hideout; the **Slickrock Divide** that is the high point between two drainage areas; **desert bighorn sheep** who were reintroduced into the park after being decimated by disease from the domestic sheep; and the oddly-shaped **hoodoos and pinnacles**. The **Scenic Drive** follows the **Capitol Gorge Spur Road**, the only road through the Waterpocket Fold until 1962. The last three miles of the road are smack dab in the bottom of the drainage and would not be a happy place in a flash flood. Make sure there are no storm clouds building in any direction before driving your rental

car into a potential dead zone! But have no fear because the Parkies closely monitor the weather radar and if there is even the slightest chance of a flash flood, they will close off the area. ***https://www.nps.gov/care/planyourvisit/scenicdrive.htm***

- At the end of the road there is a large parking area for the **Capitol Gorge Trail**. When you get out of your air-conditioned car it will probably feel like you are stepping into a blast furnace. Don't let that deter you because you will be able to find shade within the narrow gorge. And be sure to check out the excellent interpretive signs under the picnic shelter at the beginning of the trail.
- During your hike, you will see the **Pioneer Register**, where the Mormon families recorded their names on the brown canyon walls. The route you are following has been used for millennia by humans and they pecked their strange symbols onto the smooth brown canyon walls. And when the Mormon pioneers came through in the 1800s, they followed the example. Mormon pioneers tagged the walls for several hundred feet and some of the inscriptions look like they had to have been done by someone standing on a ladder because they are so high up on the rock face. ***https://utah.com/hiking/capitol-reef-national-park/capitol-gorge***
- Return to your motel and jump in the pool before cleaning up for dinner.
- Drive back toward the park on Highway 24 and pay a visit to one of my old haunts, the **Rim Rock Restaurant & Inn**. When I first visited Capitol Reef back in the early 80's, the Rimrock was the only place where you could get a hot meal. It was run by some crazy blond Hungarian B-movie star who had been in a lot of cheesy horror films. She was married to the horror movie mogul **Al Adamsen** who was killed a few years back by his contractor and buried under the hot tub at his home in Death Valley. Life imitating art, I guess. The place has undergone a major face lift and is hopping on the weekends. But have no

fear because the place is huge and can serve lots of people. It is worth waiting for a table on the back patio with its stunning views of Capitol Reef to the east. The dinners are amazing! Try the fresh trout and local asparagus. And they have an excellent selection of scotch. I strongly recommend a few wee drams of Balvenie. You earned them!

- After dinner, head back to the park to catch the **evening ranger talk** in Capitol Reef's moonlit amphitheater.
- Drive back to your hotel by the ethereal moonlight.

Best Hikes

- The **Fremont River Trail** - "Capitol Reef National Park's Fremont River Trail, named for the perennial stream it follows, ends atop a windswept hill providing sweeping views of the Waterpocket Fold, a 100-mile long wrinkle in the Earth's crust accented by a panoply of colors. The first third of the hike traverses a trail that is wide, flat, and accessible to wheelchairs, leashed pets, and bicycles. Beyond a passable wooden fence, the trail is open to hikers only. A persistent climb of 0.7 mile leads to two tremendous viewpoints – one down to the Fremont River Gorge as it cuts through pine- and juniper-studded Miners Mountain and one east to the magnificent Waterpocket Fold.

  Officially, the Fremont River Trail begins at Loop B of the **Fruita Campground**. However, non-campers can access the path by turning off the Capitol Reef Scenic Drive at the next right-hand turn beyond the campground, following signs for the amphitheater. Park at the end of the drive and connect with the trail (easy to spot) heading north; starting from the amphitheater shaves off roughly 0.2-mile round trip. (Alternatively, park at the Gifford Homestead, one mile down the Scenic Drive on the right. Walking along the riverside path between here and the campground adds 0.4-mile round trip.)

  The walk begins in the heart of historic **Fruita**, once a tiny, picturesque town founded by Mormon pioneers in the 1880s. While Fruita's population never grew larger than ten families at any given time, it became well-renowned for its fruit orchards. Apples, apricots, cherries, peaches, pears, and plums from the gardens of Fruita were sold as far as Elko, Nevada and Denver, Colorado. Upholding the tradition, the National Park Service staff at Capitol Reef maintains nearly 3,000 fruit trees today, inviting visitors to pick (and eat) as they please when the crop is ripe.

The Fremont River was – and remains – central to the orchards' survival. Fruita residents developed a series of irrigation ditches to divert water from the river (and nearby Sulphur Creek). A number of these ditches are visible along the early stretches of the hike.

Within steps of Loop B heading west, the Fremont River Trail – wide and well-packed with dirt and gravel – passes **Chestnut Orchard** (yes, that's spelled correctly), bearing mostly pear trees, on the left. To the right is the brushy river, fringed by tall grasses, green-stemmed rabbitbrush, Coyote willows, and lofty cottonwood trees (many cottonwoods are nearly as old as Fruita itself).

A couple minutes' walk reveals the back of the amphitheater on your left. At this point, visitors are greeted by a wayside exhibit previewing the hike ahead, as well as a small box containing trail brochures (available for 50 cents). From here, the trail passes the **Mulford Orchard** (mostly peaches) to the left and crosses at least two irrigation ditches – one thin and small, one significant wider and deeper. Three large cottonwoods on the right offer pleasant shade on a hot summer day.

From here it is a short walk amid thick willows and sagebrush varieties to a wooden fence, the point at which bicyclists and pet walkers must turn around. The trail continues through a hiker-width slit in the barrier.

It is approximately 100 yards to a point where the footpath begins gradually ascending the left flank of a rapidly-deepening canyon, here composed of rock from the Triassic Moenkopi formation. The climb is not overly steep, but it is a persistent slog.

Down to the right, the river has cut a rugged canyon into the golden Sinbad limestone layer of the Moenkopi. Farther upstream, older rock strata from the Permian period – Kaibab Limestone and White Rim Sandstone – are visible, forming the bottom layers of Fremont Gorge. Across the canyon, **Johnson Mesa** – an example of what's known as a strath terrace– used to form part of the valley floor, before additional down-cutting of the Fremont River and Sulphur Creek completed the landscape of today. (For a great hike across Johnson Mesa, check out the nearby Freemont Gorge Overlook Trail.

About ½ mile from the wooden fence, the trail bends to the left, skirting the rim of a side canyon. This point offers the hike's best views of **Fremont Gorge** as it snakes southwest.

The side canyon is also impressive, but the trail does not remain beside it for long. A well-trodden trail climbs steeply to a high point on the left, but the official path continues southeast to the base of the next good-sized ridge. After zig-zagging up the west-facing slope, the trail ends at a large, hiker-made cairn. Views of the Waterpocket Fold from this spot are virtually unobstructed–beginning with the red-orange Wingate sandstone cliffs to the northeast, topped by cream-colored peaks in the Navajo sandstone. Straight ahead to the east is a continuation of the Wingate cliffs, though the vertical walls here quickly give way to boulder-strewn talus slopes–and then two horizontal strips of green-gray and deep red badlands (Chinle Formation and Moenkopi Formation, respectively). Back to the west, the dip slope of **Miners Mountain** (~7,900') gradually rises to the fill the horizon, but rocky canyons add gradations to the landscape.

A little exploring – to the next ridgetop to the south – provides a better view of the Fold to the southeast, where cone-shaped **Fern's Nipple** (7,065') sits atop a wall of Wingate.

After soaking up the stunning vistas, return the way you came. The Fremont River Trail drops roughly 500 feet over the course of 0.7 mile. It is another 1/3 mile back to the amphitheater and an additional 150 yards to Loop B of the Fruita Campground."

- **From Andrew Wojtanik's blog *Live and Let Hike - An incomplete guide to hiking Utah, Colorado, Virginia, and beyond* *https://liveandlethike.com/2015/02/26 fremont-river-trail-capitol-reef-national-park-ut/***

- **The Capitol Gorge Trail** - This a short, easy up-and-back hike into a narrow gorge that follows the flat, dry streambed. Along the way you will pass petroglyphs carved by the prehistoric **Fremont Culture** until about 1300 AD. The Fremont Indians farmed along the once-flowing stream and they used this route as a highway (for walkers, of course). If it's hot, and it probably will be, just hike from shady spot to shady spot for about a mile until you came to the **Pioneer Register**. The trail continues down canyon, but it's the same as the first mile. And there is a trail up a steep, rocky, and exposed incline to **The Tanks**, some less that enticing natural depressions in the sandstone that were used by the local inhabitants to capture rainwater. I really don't think this spur trail is worth the effort, but it's only about a half-mile from the bottom of the canyon to the tanks. So, knock yourself out if you aren't too tired. Return to your car the way you came in. (2.5 miles RT) ***https://www.tripadvisor.com/Attraction_Review-g143017-d3475336-Reviews-Capitol_Gorge_Trail-Capitol_Reef_National_Park_Utah.html***

Insider Tips

- The Parkies closely monitor the weather radar and if there is even the slightest chance of a flash flood, they will close off the dangerous areas. But you should always be watching the sky for impending bad weather. And when you are hiking in a narrow canyon, take note of places where you can get to high ground if needed in an emergency.

Save Money!

- You can use the link I provide to download the **Scenic Drive map** and save yourself $2.
- Before you leave the Capitol Reef National Park Visitor Center, pick up the **FREE! park maps**, especially for the areas where you will be traveling next.

Day Thirteen

CHIMNEY ROCK, MORMON TOWNS, FISH LAKE, AND THE SALT LAKE VALLEY

Your last day on the road is going to begin with a great hike up to Chimney Rock where there are dazzling panoramic views of Capitol Reef and the mountainous world beyond. This will be a great way to start your day and end your visit to Canyonlands.

The rest of the day will be about sightseeing and driving through striking landscapes and many small Mormon towns as you work your way back to *civilization* in the Salt Lake Valley.

It's a 200-mile drive, so we are going to break up the drive by stopping at lovely vistas and storybook agricultural towns along the way.

And we are even going to throw in some majestic mountains and a lovely lake where you can stretch your legs for good measure.

You will climb through mountains and then pass through the spell-binding Koosharem Valley dotted with horses and cattle where time seems to stand still. The Cowboy Country terrain of lakes, farms, cattle ranches, lush green mountains and black volcanic fields will leave you breathless as you drive through a world of wondrous bounty and desolation. Believe it or not, you are driving through the ancient caldera of a long-extinct volcano. Much of these lands are now protected by conservation easements as the ranchers work with environmentalists to preserve the natural beauty of this forgotten part of America.

You will then drop into mining country, dominated by open pit mines and monstrous machinery where sleepy Mormon towns are busily clinging to life by harvesting the earth.

Mining will soon give way to industrial strength agriculture and the character of the towns will grow softer and more pleasant. You will stop in several of these rural waysides to catch a glimpse of life in the slow lane.

And then you will be back on Interstate 15, going 80 mph with trucks and other travelers as you close the loop back to Salt Lake City where your journey began.

Along the way you will stop in the bustling farm town of Payson to walk around the outside of their heavenly new temple that rises out of the earth like a glowing white rocket ship.

After that, it's a drive through the Utah Lake Valley, the beehive state's new technology corridor, past Spanish Fork, Springville, Provo, and Orem, where large international companies are building mega factory complexes for developing and shipping goods around the world. Companies like Amazon and Google are erecting expansive service hubs in this area, taking advantage of the well-educated and homogenously-reliable Mormon workforce. You are looking at the future of America. And it's going like gangbusters in Utah.

And you will end your day in the heart of downtown Salt Lake City, roaming the streets of this curiously sterile, but endlessly interesting, heart of the Mormon.

How to Get There

- Drive back into Capitol Reef Park and look for the trailhead for Chimney Rock on the left. (11 miles)

After your hike:

- Return to Torrey. (11 miles)

- Drive UT 24 West. (29 miles)
- Turn right onto UT 25 North to Fish Lake. (10 miles)

After your visit to Fish Lake:

- Backtrack on UT 25 to UT 24 West and turn right. (9.5 miles)
- Drive UT 24 West. (40 miles) * In the town of Sigurd, you will need to make sure you turn right to stay on UT 24.
- When you come to I-70 just past Sigurd, take I-70 west. (7 miles)
- Take the US 50 exit to the left at the **Love's Travel Stop** which will lead you into Salina.
- In the middle of Salina, continue straight onto US 89 heading north to Gunnison. (15 miles)
- In Gunnison, you will continue straight onto UT 28 north to Nephi. (41 miles)
- Get on I-15 north to Salt Lake City. (84 miles)
- Left onto US 89 North. (15 miles)

Where to Stay

- **Salt Lake Plaza Hotel** in Salt Lake City, Utah. They have an outdoor seasonal pool and offer covered parking. But they **charge for parking**. You will end up paying for parking when you visit Temple Square, so it's worth paying for the convenience of not having to look for parking. And the Salt Lake Plaza Hotel is within easy walking distance of Temple Square. ***https://www.plaza-hotel.com/en***

Camping

- **This will be your last night on the road and you will want to have a hotel room where you can shower, clean your gear, and pack for the flight home on the following day.**

Where to Eat

- Breakfast - **Capitol Reef Inn & Cafe**. They have a delectable breakfast buffet with a wide assortment of fruit and other tasty items for a very reasonable price.
- Lunch - Historic **Fish Lake Lodge** at Fish Lake ***http://www.fishlakeresorts.com/***
- Dinner - The **Garden Restaurant** in the **Joseph Smith Building**. Located on the 10th floor of the **Joseph Smith Memorial Building**, The Garden Restaurant has stunning views of Temple Square and Downtown Salt Lake City, Utah. The Garden Restaurant is "informally formal". You'll dine in a comfortable plaza-like atmosphere, surrounded by Mediterranean columns and fountains accented with live flowers and trees. This is a great place for your final dinner on your trip. You earned the luxury!
https://www.templesquare.com/dining/the-garden-restaurant/

Best Things to Do

- Eat breakfast and check out of your motel by **9AM**.
- Hike the **Chimney Rock Trail**.
- Return to Torrey and stop briefly at the **Torrey Trading Post** on your left in the middle of town by the Indian teepee.
http://www.torreytradingpost.com/
- Drive slowly through the lovely towns of **Bicknell** and **Lyman**, checking out these untouched Mormon agricultural towns that seem a bit lost out of time.
https://en.wikipedia.org/wiki/Bicknell,_Utah
https://en.wikipedia.org/wiki/Lyman,_Utah
- Drive to **Fish Lake** and continue past the lodges, restaurants, and marina to **Joe's Bush Boat Launch**. Get out and walk along the shores of the lovely alpine lake.
- Eat lunch at the historic **Fish Lake Lodge**.

- Continue your drive north to Salt Lake City.
- Go six miles past the summit on UT 24 and stop to check out the roadside attraction on the left called the **"Indian Peace Treaty Memorial**" made of colored native stone. Like Bluff Fort, it is a window into the history of how the Indians and Mormons managed to peacefully coexist with one another.
- Continue through the mountains and then pass through the ancient volcanic caldera of the spellbinding Koosharem Valley.
- Stop at **Miss Mary's Historical Museum** in Salina. This is a short, but really interesting glimpse into Utah's pioneer past. And the museum is housed in a lovely old brick building with a steeple that is worth a look even if the museum is closed.
https://www.salinacity.org/miss-marys-museum-in-salina/
- Quick stop (you can even do it from your car) in **Gunnison** to check out the impressive **City Hall** and the historic **Casino Star Theater** on the main drag.
http://www.gunnisoncity.org/
- Stop for a short hike at **Yuba Lake State Park** that will allow you to stretch your legs during the long drive. They charge **$10** to enter the park and given the short amount of time you will be visiting here, it's probably not worth it. But the entrance station is often closed, so you have a better than even chance of getting in for **FREE!**, especially on a weekday. Another option is to stay on **Temple Road** past the turnoff to the entrance of the park, turn left on **Old Yuba Dam Road**, and then park in a pull-out along the road and walk down into the park for **FREE!**
https://stateparks.utah.gov/parks/yuba/
- Stop in the bustling town of **Payson** and walk around the **outside** of the brand spanking new **Mormon Temple** (1494 South 930 West). You will see it to the right of the interstate as you are passing the town. It looks like a white interstellar rocket. Let your eyes lead you there. But **don't try and go inside because only Mormons are allowed, and even then, you need to have had a local Mormon vouch for you and then notify the folks at the Temple that you are coming**. The outside of the Temple is

well worth a brief stop. There are some lovely gardens and the grounds are open to the public.
https://ldschurchtemples.org/payson/

- Drive to Salt Lake City.
https://www.visitsaltlake.com/

- After checking into your downtown hotel, eat dinner in one of the restaurants located in the **Joseph Smith Memorial Building** which was previously the luxurious **Hotel Utah**. It houses two excellent restaurants, **The Roof Restaurant** (formal) and **The Garden Restaurant** (casual). The Roof Restaurant has fabulous vistas overlooking the **Salt Lake Mormon Temple** and is a more formal, (expensive but very delicious selections), whereas The Garden Restaurant is more reasonably priced and offers great food. The Memorial building houses many additional venues including the **LDS genealogy** facilities. The Joseph Smith Building is in the very center of downtown Salt Lake and within walking distance of Temple Square, The **Beehive House**, and many other historical sites.
https://www.templesquare.com/explore/jsmb/

- After dinner, go for a little walk. Even though you are going to visit **Temple Square** the next morning, it is definitely worth seeing at night. The nearby **State House** which you can't miss is also worth seeing when it is lit up at night.

Best Hikes

- The **Chimney Rock Trail** - This very fun hike will take you to the top of a rocky promontory along the edge of the Waterpocket Fold, providing expansive views of Capitol Reef and Boulder Mountain beyond. Chimney Rock is a natural red sandstone spire, eroded out of the side of the mesa, and stands 300 feet above the road. The trail starts on the north side of Highway 24, and quickly begins to ascend the side of the mesa, following switchbacks as the slope increases. After a steep climb, hikers find themselves at the beginning of the **Mesa Loop Trail**. When you get to the top of the mesa, the trail continues across the top of the world and then winds back down into a side canyon leading back to where you started your hike at the bottom. Once at the top, **you do not want to take the rest of the trail**. There is a short path out to Chimney Rock. Stop, rest, take in the views, and snap a few photos before heading back the way you came. (3.3 miles RT)

http://www.americansouthwest.net/utah/capitol_reef/chimney-rock-trail.html

Insider Tips

- The Torrey Trading Post will be your last best stop to pick up some Canyonlands souvenirs to take back home.
- There's a very good **pie** shop in Bicknell.
- There's an excellent **beef jerky** store in Gunnison.

Save Money!

- Fish Lake is **FREE!**
- Miss Mary's Museum in Salina is **FREE!**
- Rather than pay $10 to get into Yuba state Park, continue on Temple Road past the turnoff to the entrance of the park and then turn left on Old Yuba Dam Road. Park in a pullout along the road and walk down into the park for **FREE!**
- The Mormon Temple in Payson is **FREE!**
- Temple Square is **FREE!**

Day Fourteen

TEMPLE SQUARE & SALT LAKE CITY

How to Get There

- Walk to Temple Square.

After checking out Temple Square and the downtown area, drive to Salt Lake City Airport:

- Get on I-15 S from US-89 N/300 W/3rd W and 600 N (0.1 miles)
- Turn left at the 1st cross street onto W N Temple (0.3 miles)
- Turn right onto US-89 N/300 W/3rd W (0.7 mile)
- Turn left onto 600 N (0.6)
- Use the left 2 lanes to turn left to merge onto I-15 S toward Provo (0.4 mile)
- Take I-80 W to Terminal Dr. Take exit 115 B from I-80 W (5 miles)
- Merge onto Terminal Drive (0.3 mile)

Where to Eat

- Breakfast - **Copper Canyon Grillhouse & Tavern** in the **Radisson Hotel** just down the street on South Temple has an excellent breakfast buffet. ***https://www.tripadvisor.com/Restaurant_Review-g60922-d1454297-Reviews-Copper_Canyon_Grillhouse_Tavern-Salt_Lake_City_Utah.html***
- Lunch - **You Pick** depending where you are in the city and when your flight leaves.

Best Things to Do

- Check out **Temple Square** and the outside of the incredible **Mormon Temple**.

https://www.templesquare.com/

- **You cannot go inside the Temple**, but there are plenty of other fun attractions.
    - **Temple Square North Visitors Center**
    - **Salt Lake Tabernacle**
    - **Church History Museum**
    - **Pioneer Log Cabin**
    - **Family History Museum**
    - **Brigham Young Monument**
    - **The Beehive House**
    - **Eagle Gate**
- Check out the historic **State House**.
- Walk back to the hotel and drive to the airport.

About the Author

Steve Carr is retired and lives with his lovely wife Inna along the Chesapeake Bay in historic Annapolis, MD. He was the trails planner for the Maryland Department of Natural Resources for many years, working on developing, promoting and maintaining land trails throughout the state of Maryland.

Steve also leads unique, and very entertaining walking tours around the ancient Colonial City of Annapolis through his company "**FREE!** Annapolis Walking Tours".
http://www.bystevecarr.com/free-annapolis-walking-tours/

Over the last twenty years, Steve has managed many successful Annapolis and state political campaigns while implementing a wide range of environmental projects throughout the Annapolis area. Steve is a leading expert on local government issues, lecturing throughout the Chesapeake Bay region on a wide variety of topics.

Steve is a captivating public speaker and is in much demand. For those interested in booking a speaking engagement, Steve can be reached on Facebook, Twitter, or at:

steve.carr567@gmail.com

In 2008, Steve authored the very popular book about the Chesapeake Bay entitled ***"Water Views"***, a collaboration with famed Bay photographer Marion Warren and celebrated "Capital" cartoonist Eric Smith.

In 2010, Steve published ***"The Canyon Chronicles"***, a surreal memoir of intrigue and misadventure covering his fifteen years working for the U.S. Forest Service on the Kaibab National Forest on the North Rim of the Grand Canyon.

In 2012, Steve published ***"Anasazi Strip"***, the first book in the **Jenny Hatch Mystery Series**.

In 2014, Steve published ***"Kachina Roulette"***, the second book in the **Jenny Hatch Mystery Series**. "Kachina Roulette" is fast becoming a popular favorite with Southwest fans of Tony Hillerman, Edward Abbey, and Hunter S. Thompson.

In 2016, Steve published his first in a series of guidebooks entitled ***"Best of the Southwest - The Grand Circle"***.
http://www.bystevecarr.com/my-books/

Steve also has a regular column in ***"Bay Weekly"*** where he tackles natural curiosities, environmental issues of the day, and world class sailing events like the Volvo Ocean Race.

Steve is an avid world traveler and outdoorsman who bikes (He rode his bicycle twice across the United States!), kayaks, sails, hikes, golfs, and hashes in his spare time with his lovely wife Inna.

You can find links to all of Steve's books and follow Steve's adventures on his popular travel blog at:
http://www.bystevecarr.com/